MAN ALIVE

A True Story of Violence, Forgiveness and Becoming a Man

Thomas Page McBee

City Lights Books | San Francisco

Cover art: "Beefcake Paperdoll," a painting by Xavier Schipani

This book is also available in an e-edition: 978-0-87286-624-9

Library of Congress Cataloging-in-Publication Data
McBee, Thomas Page.
Man alive : a true story of violence, forgiveness and becoming a man / Thomas Page McBee.
pages cm — (City lights/sister spit)
ISBN 978-0-87286-624-9 (paperback)
1. McBee, Thomas Page. 2. Transsexuals—United States—Biography. 3. Transgender people—United States—Biography. 4. Female-to-male transsexuals—United States--Biography. 5. Gender identity—United States. I. Title.

HQ77.8.M385A3 2014
306.76'8092—dc23
[B]

2014022173

This is a work of nonfiction, but it relies on memory and, as such, its attendant illusions, specters, and plays of light. It is the truth as I've lived it. Many names have been changed.

City Lights Books are published at the City Lights Bookstore
261 Columbus Avenue, San Francisco, CA 94133
www.citylights.com

PRAISE FOR *MAN ALIVE*

"Thomas McBee's *Man Alive* hurtled through my life. I read it in a matter of hours. It's a confession, it's a poem, it's a time warp, it's a brilliant work of art. I bow down to McBee—his humility, his sense of humor, his insightfulness, his structural deftness, his ability to put into words what is often said but rarely, with such visceral clarity and beauty, communicated."—Heidi Julavits, author of *The Vanishers* and *The Uses of Enchantment*

"*Man Alive* is a sweet, tender hurt of a memoir. Thomas Page McBee deftly recounts what has shaped him into the man he has become and how—from childhood trauma to a mugging in Oakland where he learned of his body's ability to save itself. This is a memoir about forgiveness and self-discovery, but mostly it's about love, so much love. McBee takes us in his capable hands and shows us what it takes to become a man who is gloriously, gloriously alive."—Roxane Gay, author of *Bad Feminist* and *An Untamed State*

"Thomas Page McBee's story of how he came to claim both his past and his future is by turns despairing and hopeful, exceptional and relatable. To read it is to witness the birth of a fuller, truer self. I loved this book."—Ann Friedman, columnist, *New York Magazine*

"Reading *Man Alive* is like sitting with someone uncurling his hands, then holding them out to you, open, so that you can behold all the hard-won strength, insight, agility, and love to be found there. 'Whoever's child I am, my body belongs to me,' McBee writes, and his book is an elegant, generous transcription of the journey toward this incandescent, non-aggrandized, life-sustaining form of self-possession—the kind that emanates from dispossession, rather than running from it."—Maggie Nelson author of *Bluets* and *The Art of Cruelty: A Reckoning*

"Following a twisty course marked by multiple switchbacks, *Man Alive* picks its path through a life pocked by abuse, yearning, violence, danger and desire. The book refuses to cleave to the conventions of other narratives of transition and makes uncertainty the hallmark not only of the past but of the present and the future as well. Exquisitely written and bristling with emotion, this important book reminds us of how much vulnerability and violence inheres to any identity. A real achievement of form and narrative."—Jack Halberstam, author of *The Queer Art of Failure*

"*Man Alive* isn't just a story about a transgender man. It's a story about self-discovery. It's a story about patience, forgiveness, kindness and bravery. It's a story told so beautifully and clearly that you can't help but see your own journey in these pages. With this book, Thomas Page McBee has done exactly what we should all strive for: to tell our stories in ways that humanize rather than sensationalize."—Lauren Morelli, writer, *Orange Is the New Black*

For you, whoever you are.

prologue

South Carolina

August 2010 • 29 years old

What makes a man?

It's not that I haven't studied them: their sinew, their slang, their beautiful bristle; but before I was held at gunpoint on a cold April day, I couldn't have told you.

A real man, a family man, the Marlboro man, man up.

The man in the mirror.

I loved that Michael Jackson song, growing up. Used to forget my girl-hips, used to sing it to my best imagination of myself.

What makes a man? The need to know led me to my father's hometown in hot-damp South Carolina. The story starts there because that's where I went when I could no longer afford to leave the question alone, to let it rear up every few years, when I'd had too much to drink and it was just me and my reflection and my hungry ghosts. And so I steered my rental through the swampy South with my cap pulled low. I had that teen-boy swagger, scars like smiles across my chest, and a body I was just beginning to love.

But the story also begins the night I almost died, back in April of 2010. And in 1985, when my father became a monster, and in 1990 when my mom found out he was one.

"Men," she'd said then. And I'd learned to say it the same way, a lemon in my mouth.

In South Carolina I could smell it through my open window: alligators and secrets; the embers of Sherman's march, the Klu Kux Klan, my father's farm, burning. It smelled like my animal fear and the spicy deodorant I used to cover it.

Men, I thought with that old bitterness, but I already knew my body was shifting. In fact that's why I was there.

A good man is hard to find.

The windshield blurred; the road was inky, the rain biblical. The cheap motel off the highway seemed like not such a hot idea after I passed my fifth gun-racked pick-up, but there wasn't any turning back.

Once a body is in motion, it stays in motion. My mom's a physicist; she told me that.

The truth is, this is a ghost story. No, this is an adventure story.

This is an adventure story about how I quit being a ghost.

I

Freeze

1 Oakland

April 2010 • 29 years old

Here's what you need to know about Parker: she *hummed* with a magic that vibrated her long strides, her quick-wit, her dressings-down. Though softened by Southern manners, her mood could turn sharp as a knife's edge, and it wasn't too hard to find yourself on the sticking side of it. I'd seen her make a cat-caller wither and call a real dick of a roommate a piece of shit, repeatedly, until he just sort of disappeared, his stuff packed and gone within the month.

It was like loving a hurricane.

That night she was wound-up, the plastic bag with a new pair of shoes tossed over her shoulder. We'd spent the day in San Francisco, bumming around and seeing a play neither of us cared much for—something about three generations of women—it felt like those sorts of plays were always about three generations of women. As we left the BART station and headed to our neighborhood in Oakland, Parker outlined her issue with associating women with domesticity in the sort of hilariously acidic free-association tirade she'd go on just for kicks.

She was in her French New Wave phase, and it suited her: short hair, shirts thick with nautical stripes. She looked like Jean Seberg in *Breathless*, her blue eyes big as saucers. She could be merciless in her assessments, but beneath that lay a kindness so clear it was almost painful to observe. I squeezed her hand, and she startled into holding my gaze.

"What?" she asked.

I shook my head. Six years in, she knew.

Mostly, she was a smart-ass. "I have an opinion on everything," she'd say.

"How about whales?" I'd ask.

"Love them! Key to the ecosystem; smart."

I'd try to think of the most innocuous, boring subject. "Row houses?"

"Depressing in brick, cute in wood."

Parker also had strong opinions about walking home so late at night, and I knew why: our friend who discovered a man under her bed, our friend who was bound to a chair during a home invasion, our friend who got punched in the face in broad daylight for no good reason.

That night was the worst kind of foggy: you could breathe it in, feel it stick. I pulled my collar up, my hat down, my hood on. We walked because we were too broke to take a cab, because we couldn't afford to be afraid and for me that meant being fearless, and mostly because she was in a good mood and I'd convinced her to.

We started down 40th, and I ignored my twitchy heart, and walked tall. If I'd learned anything since I was a kid, it was that if I wanted my life to start, I needed to show up for it.

Foolish, maybe, but I'd peacock through a warzone before I'd admit to that twitch.

2 Pittsburgh

1990 • 10 years old

"You can tell me anything," Mom said, her eyes wide, a flush creeping up her neck. Her cursive was bubbly, effervescent, recording everything I said. *1985–1990.* The dates, she said, were for her records.

I told her, then, about Dad's fingers in the pool, in the car on the way to her brother's funeral, Sunday afternoons when she left for the grocery store and he parked Ellie and Scott in front of the television, when he knew no one would come for me. Ellie and Scott and I were each two years apart but it seemed we lived in three different houses then, with three different Moms and Dads, each of us in separate, abutting childhoods.

Mine was chocolate milk, science fairs, camping, and the rituals that kept Dad's hot breath distinct from the rest of it. I sat on the floor of the closet and threw shoes at the wall. I ran like a deer through the woods behind my house. I picked one tiny thing to look forward to and fixated on it. From his bedspread I jumped into tomorrow and felt the soccer ball connect with my foot and fly, high and sweet, into the corner of the net.

There are the facts of what happened, but the story is in parts. It is still hard to capture the salty terror of the worst of it, the freeze, the split: how I lost a body, or how I conflated the two ways my body was lost to me.

I was born female, that's a fact. I saw myself as a boy, but that made a certain kind of sense. It wasn't until much later that the complex facts of my anatomy needled at me. Later, people would say that my manhood was always there, blueprinted in my torn-knee jeans, my He-Man castle, my short hair. Maybe that's true, but let's not make this the kind of story where I know all the answers.

What you need to know is that afterwards I'd read a book in my bathtub, and my little legs, hands, torso would return to me eventually, and that was what it meant to be alive: clean and immersed in a library book I could make sense of, breathing in the sharp smell of soap, touching the warm boundary of my skin to the scratchy bottom of the tub.

I never felt lonely when I had the damp pages of *Great Expectations* to keep me company, but I couldn't expect anyone to understand the way my body spangled back to life when I saw myself in Pip's tragic, romantic hope. I admired his dogged faith, even in failure. I liked that he believed in something. Mom called me Pip for years, but I never knew if we saw the same resemblance. After my transition, she'd call me "sweet boy" once, uncharacteristically, and I'd realize that maybe the similarity, for her, had been as simple as that.

I didn't tell Mom about the bathtub ritual, intuiting that to do so would encourage the cloak of guilt to hood her eyes, making her spooky and deaf to me. I didn't want her to go mix herself a strong screwdriver and leave the lamp off in the failing light.

Instead, I allowed her translation of the story to go forward in blue ink as her hand moved assuredly across the notebook pages, sheaths of paper stacked neatly into a folder she said she'd use to ensure that we were never left wanting. I didn't understand it then, but we were sinking into bankruptcy, and she wanted to keep my father tethered to us. This was her version of vigilante justice, protecting us financially by hanging the threat of this story over him. In the end, it wouldn't be my story but my silence that would keep me, all of us, alive.

"Just tell me the truth," she'd said, but I knew even then that most people don't mean that exactly, so I didn't tell her about the day in the living room, the way I retched, the terrible taste of him and the way I washed my mouth with soap and water but never got clean.

I stared out the window into the trees beside our house, my knees scratched and my brain pulsating in a stinging drone. *In 10 years, I'll be okay,* I promised myself. Ten years seemed impossibly far away, double my lifetime, but something to hitch my hope to. My heart felt strung up in my chest. Panic choked me whenever I met Mom's eyes: she looked like a stranger. Beyond her, the house seemed tilted and too bright. I'd had a life of poetry and swim meets despite my father's searching hands, and now I wasn't sure what, exactly, I was about to lose.

"I hate him," she announced, startling me out of the gauzy silence. I nodded, but didn't respond. I couldn't explain to either of us why I didn't.

"Try to remember the first time it happened," I heard her say, her voice businesslike, as if she were quizzing me ahead of a math test. "You can tell me anything," she added again, softening her tone.

I couldn't help but think of the photographs I'd taken all summer of sticky stray dogs with matted fur and scabbed noses. The world seemed to me a place of beautiful, damaged things and I wanted to love them all.

I fiddled with my shoelaces and met my mom's gaze. I felt movement in my ragged chest, a whole flock of birds gearing up to depart. I let myself go.

"I was four," I began. "At the old house."

I sounded like someone else. I didn't know how to translate the calm alongside the fear, to explain that afterwards I'd remind myself that I was stronger than him, that I could contain all of that wildness and terror until it was hard and small, until it sparked like a firework in my gut, until I could find something lovely in its wake.

I watched her face bunch in pained concentration as I spoke about where and when and how he touched me. I felt like a marionette, otherworldly and wooden, as I watched her transcribe each sentence, letting my eyes slowly cross until the letters blurred together, until the words quit being my own.

3

Oakland

April 2010 • 29 years old

Somehow, despite the sweaty wool cap pulled to my eyebrows and the Carhartt jacket zipped tight across my flat chest, despite the swagger in my walk and the way I'd pitched my voice, still the hostess at the fancy Spanish place on Valencia Street had called me "ma'am." She'd tossed the word over her shoulder like a grenade as she led Parker and me to the table by the window, and though it had been hours I ruminated darkly on every detail of my outfit: where had I gone wrong? I didn't need her to look at my narrow face and slim frame and see a man exactly, but how could she think "woman"?

Parker was tired of this conversation. It made her antsy. She was annoyed by the late hour, now frustrated by the choice we'd made not to take a smelly cab that last mile home from the BART station, the sheen of foggy cold sticking to her face.

"I hate it here," she announced.

"I know." I thought of the woman's pleased expression, how much easier it might be to live someplace that wasn't a stronghold of lesbians with short hair and big biceps, a place where the beginnings of laugh lines or the slight flare of my hips wouldn't tip anyone to the fact that I wasn't a teenage boy.

A black plastic bag stuck to the chain-link fence surrounding the BART's parking lot fluttered, its crinkle the only noise on the street. The hairs rose on my arms as a skateboarding teen rattled past us. Up ahead, a college-age woman walked alone, headphones on, easy prey.

"You think she's going to be okay?" I asked, suspecting myself of sexism.

"As okay as anybody is," Parker said, her look confirming it. "Let's cross."

We'd always head over to 41st because 40th was the dicier street, more shuttered foreclosures despite the brand-new mac-'n-cheese restaurant and fancy bike store.

Once we passed the sad donut shop in the sagging old strip mall we turned toward the single-family homes and new condos of 41st. I couldn't shake my unease, the fog niggling its way under the collar of my flannel shirt. Balls and garden tools lay abandoned in front yards, tricycles knocked on their sides as if everybody had already fled what I was just beginning to sense.

I knew something in my body: a sharp, growing buzz. I heard him before I saw him: light footfalls, too fast.

We turned to look, like two sea birds facing a tsunami. We were all of us at the four-way stop, as he walked away from 40th and the girl I'd worried for. He wore no earphones, carried no bag. He was just a silhouette in a black hoodie under the broken streetlight. I saw his face, fleetingly, in passing—handsome, a little crazed—and then Parker and I crossed and continued up 41st, leaving him behind us.

I told myself not to be weird.

I loved Parker's no-nonsense stride; she'd moved like that since college. She'd learned to carry a knife in her boot, to throw a punch; she prided herself on her unfailing competency, and it was all there, in that walk.

I could hear him moving in rhythm with her. Something about his gait bothered me: it was direct, too contained, too hurried for an empty street. The neighborhood sounds receded, the televisions and barking dogs. A tiny bell rang a warning: *Run*, it said.

I ignored it. Parker. I tried to focus, this was important. I loved her for more than the knife in her boot. I loved her for the ways she was when no one else was looking, and I wish I'd said it, I'd meant to say it, but

I was shoved, my teeth clattering,
Parker, turning toward me
hands like hot irons on my shoulders, I
flew and I was
released.

4 Pittsburgh

1990 • 10 years old

"Your dad's a bad man," Mom said, studying herself in the bathroom mirror. I watched from the stairs of the walk-in closet, the light a sickly glow through the tightened blinds beside the tub. She was beautiful in an offbeat way: chunky purple necklaces, thin brown hair, infectious cackle. She applied her mysterious makeup, rouges and liners and then hair spray, a noxious cloud. She was a scientist used to being the only woman in a room, or on Air Force Two, briefing Ted Kennedy on structural physics; at General Electric, taking the wives out to dinner so they didn't think she had designs on their husbands.

"He wants to apologize," she told me, painting a purple on her eyelids the color of our summer sunsets in North Carolina. I felt myself disappear, thinking instead about upturned buckets of sand and crabs we'd caught ourselves for supper, dangling ropes strung with slimy turkey necks off the dock.

She turned to me and I made my face neutral. I hated her concern, and how much I wanted it.

I used to imagine a car accident when she'd leave for the grocery store and Dad would come for me. At her funeral, everyone would hold me gently while I cried. Feeling guilty at the memory, I watched her watch me, saw myself in her round cheeks and Slavic nose, but not the silky pleats of her dress or the wet mist of her Chanel bottle with the little black pump.

What I had were questions. Like: how could the distant, sleazy man who pressed himself against me then break through the weird blankness of his eyes to help me build a model engine that same night? Do we all have two people inside of us?

I mean, do I?

Mom stopped brushing her hair, and I felt the tremble in the room. If the story were up to me, she'd never cry. "I just want you to have a normal childhood," she said, pulling me close, her breath minty, her belly warm, her fear in what she didn't say, wouldn't say but I knew it anyway: that she worried for me, that she stayed up at night convincing herself it wasn't already too late.

◆

I could tell that Dad charmed people. Everyone gravitated to his lilting Southern accent, his aw-shucks smile and his good manners. He seemed youthful, refined, and so it was easy to overlook his silver halo, forget that he was in his fifties, way older than Mom.

But people can hold their true selves at bay for only so long—I knew that from *Batman*. Today, he looked worn out, exposed, waiting for us in the leather chair, his remaining hair unkempt, gray stubble crowding his face. His knuckles were thick, swollen as an old man's, and he wore his exercise clothes: a gray tracksuit, coffee-stained.

He looked like the raggedy dog he'd once shot in the butt with a BB gun for crossing onto our property one too many times. "What are you doing?" Mom had said on the sunny porch that afternoon a few years before, her voice laced with alarm; maybe she'd never seen that side of him, but I knew it intimately, and how he'd look when he turned around, smiling that dumb, menacing smile. Of course one man can become another. Where two sides meet comes the potential for ghosts: dissonant smears, rips in the story.

"It was only his ass," he'd said in that gentle accent, unloading the BBs carefully into his palm. "Just teaching him a lesson."

The dog never did come back.

◆

Today he wasn't that man or the model-engine one; he was even worse, in a way: more desperate, primal. "I'm very sorry," he said, his head bowed.

We all faced each other like sacks of skin.

"My parents would've been so disappointed in me," he added, oddly. There was a tremble in his voice. "I'm sorry to you, to them, to your mom." He sniffed.

Somehow, I felt worse in the living room than I had the whole time he'd hurt me. *Hurt*, that's what the therapist called it. All of these adults choosing the wrong words, missing the language, missing me.

When he wasn't holding me down on a bed, I was hauling around the junky camcorder, dressing up the neighborhood kids and making horror movies with ketchup and bald-head caps. Or I was building a fort in the woods, a hiding spot with books and a flashlight, dried fruit, cookies.

What he did didn't hurt. It disconnected, it made two

of me like there were two of him. It made me a stranger to myself.

"I'm sorry," he said. "You don't deserve—"

I tried to figure out what he was apologizing for.

"I never meant—," he said and leaned into his hands, choking on his own soggy snot.

Shut up shut up shut up, I thought. I gave him a look like he gave that dog, and he did.

5 Oakland

April 2010 • 29 years old

I crashed to the sidewalk. My palm bled a little, my body vibrated with ghost hands and a dark hum of a different time.

"Up," the man attached to the fists said.

I pushed myself off the concrete, moved to the balls of my feet.

"Not all the way up!" he barked.

I froze, arms raised, my back to him, on my knees.

"Turn around."

I pivoted clumsily. His eyes were warm, kind even, but spastic. His hands were deep in the kangaroo pocket of his sweatshirt. He towered—Darth Vader with a goatee.

"Stay down," he whispered, raw like a scream.

Shut up shut up shut up, I thought.

Parker, all lean muscle, appeared behind him just then, a miracle, her bag aimed at his skull. She'd gone head-to-head with a shitty stepdad for most of her teens, and as she cocked her arm back I thought, briefly, that we might have a chance.

He sensed her and, turning with the grace of a ballet dancer, pulled a handgun from his kangaroo pocket and motioned her downward. She dropped, and the scene bent into a posed tableau: me on my knees with empty eyes, the gun extended toward us, and Parker's mouth with her snaggletooth poking out, forming a tight "O" as she crouched into herself, knowing what I know, what I wish she'd never had to learn: how to disappear.

He turned back to me, his mouth moving in slow motion. My heartbeat grew sluggish, I could hear it *ca-thunk, ca-thunk*.

I felt warm, full of energy and particles. It was almost spiritual, but for the familiar haze, the awareness that I was splitting, abandoning myself to a gun and a mumbling man.

Come back, I thought.

He kneeled down beside me. I focused on the whites of his eyes, his teeth. I smelled dog shit, exhaust, dirty clothes. I wiggled my toes dully. Nothing.

The air was electric with his strange frustration, the waving gun. I handed him my wallet and he threw it to the ground. I looked for Parker but all I saw was her crouching shadow.

I couldn't move and I couldn't even think, except to note, dully, that I was immobilized, a bystander to my own story.

6
Pittsburgh
1990 • 10 years old

"Crocodile tears," Mom said the day after Dad apologized. I didn't know what that meant, but it made me picture him slithering toward me, so I shut my eyes.

"I could just cut his brakes," she said, nodding toward his sedan in the airless garage. We were in the van beside it, underneath a swinging light cord. I stared at his car like it might rear up to defend itself.

Here's a story I don't remember: in the bathroom, I told my red hairbrush about Dad. Had I wanted someone to hear? Sometimes we are mysteries, even to ourselves. My live-in babysitter walked by, pressed her ear to the door. She'd held me like a big, gangly baby and asked careful questions in her honey voice.

"Try to forgive him," she'd said on the last day I ever saw her, holding my hand and fingering the cross around her neck.

"She must have felt guilty," Mom sighed when Susan left in the middle of the night, speeding off in her sporty Mazda. A loneliness settled in my chest. I was an astronaut, floating farther and farther away.

The truth was, I kind of wanted Mom to kill him. I watched her in the half-light, knowing she wouldn't. I thought that no one could really ever forgive anyone, and

I looked at her face: unfamiliar, trembling, clenched. I worried the hole in the knee of my jeans. What would a normal kid say?

"Maybe you'd get in trouble?" I offered. She looked at me, her face crumpling.

"Hey," she said, pulling my hand away from the fraying fabric. "You're safe now." We were quiet for a minute, but I thought about the scramble of words: how if you repeat something enough times, the meaning disappears.

Safe, I thought. *Safesafesafesafesafesafesafesafesafesafe*.

7

Oakland

April 2010 • 29 years old

The way the mugger looked through me, I knew he was gripped by that same zombie energy that had made my father's eyes go vacant, and that's what tipped me to the fact that I could die. People die every day for less.

The part of me still present, the part that wanted to move, saw another truth: everyone still had a chance. Parker could run, Vader could let us go, Dad could be a different man, I could live.

Down on 40th, a car honked an irritated staccato, breaking the spell. Vader grabbed my bag and skittered a few feet off, clutching it to his chest.

Wake up wake up wake up. I felt the pain radiating waves from my knees, the bruises forming.

Several blocks away, headlights began to make their dull way toward us through the fog. Vader studied the car's approach with agitation, turned toward it and then away. "Don't move," he warned, backing away with the gun trained on me, not Parker.

The headlights grew brighter. Suddenly he was back, a blast of stale-smelling clothes. He grabbed my collar, dragged me from the sidewalk into the bushes of the side street, under the broken lamp. I could finally see Parker, just a couple of feet away. Her eyes, blue and green, met mine. The fear in them was disorienting.

That's not a real gun, I tried to tell her without words.

"Stay," he said. He crossed the street just as the car approached, and then ducked behind a parked truck.

We should run, I thought dreamily.

The car slowed, the tires sticky on the damp pavement. Vader had miscalculated the scope of its headlights and I found myself illuminated, hallelujah, on my knees on a residential street, blinking into the light.

I held my breath and shook out a little wave. The car lingered for a minute, mid-intersection. I gestured one more time, the ache of my knees surfacing again into my consciousness, my back pulsing, my body thawing back into place.

I listened for Vader as I'd learned to do with my father, but all was still beneath the sound of the Volvo's rough engine.

I closed my eyes and the car squealed off, a spooked horse.

No one will rescue you, I told myself. Somewhere far away, a siren screamed into the night.

8 Pittsburgh

1990 • 10 years old

"The police chief's here to talk to you," Mom said. I was alone in my room, still trying to build the model engine Dad bought me, but it was way harder without his help. For a brief moment I imagined she'd actually killed him while I slept, but I could hear the distant sound of the riding mower and smell the cut grass through my window.

The police chief reeked of Old Spice, Dad's aftershave, and I disliked him immediately. Anyone could be a molester, I knew: Mom had grown increasingly suspicious of friends' fathers, even relatives.

Every man could turn, like sour milk.

I was obedient, keeping track of who to tell what, how to behave. But I hadn't been briefed on a police chief, on what sort of truth he might require. I looked at Mom, but she just gave me the same sad expression he did.

He sat at our dining room table, sleeves rolled up, a half-smile under his mustache. A recorder sat like an insect between us on the table in front of me. I didn't like the way his hair crowned his head, didn't like his straight teeth or his scruff.

"Your mom wanted you to tell us what happened—" he seemed unsure of how to go on, and I didn't like that, either. The worst thing in the world was a nervous adult.

"That's right," Mom said, providing no further clues. I kept my eyes down as he launched into questions, my cheeks reddening with each one. I knew the recorder trapped me in this stupid story, this truth.

How often, he asked. What would Dad say about telling Mom? Where were Ellie and Scott? Where did he touch you?

Then it was finally done, the words stamped on tape, no time to sculpt something less bleak. The house was full of ghosts. But wait.

"I need to ask you one more thing: something very important," he paused, and my stomach dropped in excitement, anxiety. No one asked me important anything. "And think about it carefully, because it's a big decision."

Mom looked at him expectantly. I flexed my bicep, felt the muscle under the cotton of my shirt.

"You can say whatever you want, no one will be mad, okay?" He leaned toward me, the smell of him a five-alarm mix of sweat and cologne. I moved back, nauseous. Maybe that's the reflex that spun the story in another direction: fear as propellant, the foreign smell of a man's hot breath on my face.

"Do you want your dad to go to prison?"

Everything froze.

◆

A diorama: our babysitter, somewhere far from us in her convertible Mazda Miata, her auburn hair extended in all directions; Dad still outside in his heavy work gloves, his heart thundering at the sight of the cruiser; Mom's eyes on mine, the story she'd told me about why he still lived with us: bankruptcy, property taxes, a fruitless job hunt, something something something.

I knew, better than I knew myself, what my family needed me to do.

"No," I said.

I watched another part of me fly away.

He gave me a look, an adult expression that Mom called "tired."

"Are you sure?"

A story in motion stays in motion. I nodded, and he waited for me to say more, but my silence was my language, my silence eclipsed truth until it became it.

Oakland

April 2010 • 29 years old

Vader reappeared as soon as the car blew past me, and I felt the weather change: he was more spastic, desperate. He whispered to me, his eyes the color of the hardwood floors of our old Victorian on Broad Street, the bedroom of sneaked cigarettes and first kisses.

Something something give me, he mumbled. The gun held forth like the queen of the sky.

"Here," Parker interrupted, waving her wallet. He ignored her, his eyes barely moving from mine.

"You can use my credit cards," she went on in a measured tone I'd never heard before, soothing and forced. She'll never be the same, I thought.

He took a step back and grabbed the wallet out of her hand.

"Okay?" she said, and then looked at me, like *come on.*

Wake up.

I have no cash—

I was mute. I hadn't actually spoken, I realized. Not once. "You can take my credit cards," I parroted Parker. My voice struck me, as it always did, as reedy: womanly.

Something passed over his face, his eyes focusing in on me. He shook his head like, *Fuck.* There was a wail of pain in my knees, an eruption of pins and needles in my hands and feet. He lowered the gun.

"Run," he said, a mercy so abrupt, I barely heard it.

But my body knew exactly what to do. Shedding ghost hands, I came back to life and launched into the night like a rocketship, trailing a streaming cloud of my breath.

Pittsburgh

1990 • 10 years old

I ran past Dad on his riding lawnmower, wearing his dumb blue mesh hat. In the woods, behind the patch of maples, was my oak tree with its elephant-skin bark. I lay out on the huge, fallen trunk, watching the sun twinkle through a canopy of dead leaves.

I listened for the tight smack of the police chief's car door, but all I heard were birds, calling to each other, *I'm alive I'm alive.* I missed Ellie and Scott, who had taken to playing together alone, sensing something toxic about me in the way that children do.

I pictured the house from above: Mom on her way back to her bedroom with a vodka and orange juice; Dad watching the police chief leave from high up on his mower; Scott and Ellie in their shared bathroom mixing baby powder and Mom's perfumes into poisonous lotions, their little faces scrunched in concentration.

Slap the cover closed, story's over: the babysitter drove on, the police chief gave Dad the stink eye and sighed, Dad put some fuel in his lawnmower and opened the throttle. Mom looked at herself in the mirror, but I don't know, will never know, what anyone else sees there.

Much later she called my name and I didn't answer,

didn't flinch when I heard footsteps crashing through the leaves, not caring who came for me.

◆

Because I told myself this story: I know how to be invisible, untouchable. I could put my body to sleep, limb by limb. I could wait a lifetime, if I had to, to wake up.

11

Oakland

April 2010 • 29 years old

My ears popped and a rush of sounds blew in: the smack of our feet as we ran, a wet cough, the slam of a closing window, the vibrating bass of a car stereo, irritated barking, tires on asphalt. We ran for blocks, barely noticing the passing jumble of porch swings, rock gardens, lawn ornaments.

I could have lifted a car, saved a baby pinned under its metal casings. The pinpricks in my limbs subsided, everything waking simultaneously. I sensed it: a portal opening. I felt myself waver for a moment between selves, all of them present: the child, the body I'd always been, and the one I would become.

I looked back at the empty street. "He's gone," I said, slowing a little, and Parker nodded but kept her eyes straight ahead. We moved in tandem past a fixed-gear bike chained to a wooden porch, past dark windows, past scooters and yard sale signs stapled to telephone poles.

Everything was sharp: the cobalt blue of the car beside me, the heat pouring off me, the smell of pavement.

"Are you okay?" I asked Parker, who grimaced with every step. Her pupils were huge, her face blank. Ahead of us, on the left, I saw movement in the leathery front seat of a parked Mercedes; a woman's hands, the visor down, lighting the interior like a beacon.

"Stop," I said. "Parker!" She looked back at me where I stood motioning at the car, like she wasn't sure she could speak. He could be anywhere, I thought darkly, the victory of escape dwindling as I came to a full stop. Parker's forehead was shiny with sweat. "Parker?" I asked, but she stayed quiet.

"Parker?" I wanted to tell her to get back in her body, to resist the freeze. "Hey," I said, grabbing her hand. "We're alright, okay?"

She nodded blankly, a little tremble in her lip. "Help," I nodded toward the parked car.

"Okay," she said, finally, her voice flat.

"You're okay," I said, grateful for once for the sound of myself. Something about my voice in the tick-tock eyes of this man had given me a new story where being female kept me safe.

I banged on the passenger side of the Mercedes, a storm of fists on the startled woman's window. She rolled it down slowly to a winking slit.

"We've been mugged," I said. Her hair was dark, her eye shadow heavy. I met her eyes, the way I'd learned to in a psych class in college. "He has a gun. He's behind us."

"Oh," she searched our faces, assessing. She wasn't much older than us, I realized, 35 tops. But she appeared ageless, her hair sleek and short, her blouse expensive, her skin wrinkled from laughing or smoking or both. "Okay, oh god; of course. Come on, I live here," she pointed to a condo, one of the new ones, the ones we'd derided for their tacky, soulless gentrification vibe, big flat-screens displayed through picture windows. Parker stared dumbly at her and I fixed my jaw shut, willing myself not to cry as she pushed open the front door.

It was the carpet that undid me, heartbreakingly gentle under my feet. I could hear the wild whinny of my own sob, and it scared me. Parker reached for me and I fell against her, while the woman ducked quietly up her stairs, leaving us to it.

"You could have died," Parker said softly, finally, her face wet as mine. I nodded. She smelled of jasmine and salt. I forgot the gun, and Vader, and the stillness; I wiped my nose on the back of my hand and thought, instead, about the running, how good it felt to escape on my own legs, to be one with my body.

"Ready?" Parker asked, getting some color back.

She could have been asking about anything.

"Yes," I said, meaning all of it.

II Flight

12

South Carolina

August 2010 • 29 years old

The rain came in torrents and I let the wipers push the mess of water back and forth, let the sound remind me of how small I was. I tried to locate, as I had in the months between the mugging and this trip to South Carolina, the moment I had sprung back to life. I kept coming back to the mugger's mercy, the marvel I'd felt at my body's mechanics, the night air in my lungs, the running an earthquake opening the earth beneath me and yet also a winged possibility, soaring above the shaky ground.

I'd been running ever since: long, sweaty loops around my neighborhood, trying to get that kite-feeling back. When I couldn't find it, I knew I needed to run farther still.

Which is how I found myself in the soupy South, driving toward a too-cheap motel, past mattress store billboards and scripture PSAs, following the logic of my hammering heart despite the twinge in Parker's smile at the airport drop-off.

At least she hadn't fought me on it, and I was glad to not have to explain my sense that something tremendous was at work, a grace I was too scared to name—worried I'd sound lost, or worse, religious.

Ghost hunting, I'd told her, as if that were any explanation. I wanted to see where my father grew up, to hear family stories, to try to figure out the anatomy of his freeze, why he hadn't broken out of it, why he'd always come for me with glazed eyes, what made him and me different.

So I'd packed a bag, got on the plane, not admitting until I was in the air that doing so was a matter of survival.

◆

Once a body is in motion, it stays in motion.

Since the mugging, a bearded version of myself ran shirtless through my dreams. I'd awaken energized and damp with sweat, as if I were actually thawing. Slick and a little seasick, I'd get out of bed and force myself to really see my hips, my smooth skin and narrow jaw. My chest, flat from the top surgery I'd had two years ago, no longer looked like a proud distinction of androgyny.

I looked like a blank slate, waiting.

A good man is hard to find, I thought, turning in to the dingy motel parking lot. I made my mouth serious, told myself to remember to look everyone in the eye. Then I slung my bag over my shoulder and walked real slow past three stringy-haired hunters with bloody coolers standing sentry by the sliding glass doors.

Fear fluttered my chest and I let it; I listened to its song. The guys eyed me in my fitted white T-shirt and tight jeans and tattoos. I knew they thought I was gay, or—I couldn't decide which was scarier—they'd read me as not-male. They fell silent as I drew closer, their hands shoved in pockets, a council of crows watching me pass into the building.

Keep going, something in me said, something more beautiful than a ghost. My knees, in their holiness, carried me on.

Alligators and secrets; chlorine and dog. I pulled my

cap down low and hoped for the best as I gave the weaselly guy in the fluorescent light my credit card, my girl-name stamped clearly across the front.

He looked a beat too long before handing me my key.

"There's a bar across the street, sir," he said, handing the card back to me. I didn't like the knowing tone of his voice, so I just nodded and turned away, remembering that the sound of my voice was still enough to change the story.

13

South Carolina

August 2010 • 29 years old

I put my bags down, lay on the scratchy comforter, and tried to steady myself. "Run," I could hear the mugger say, over and over, like a slow-motion sports reel; I could marker a circle around my knees and write: "Here's where I stopped playing dead."

"The mugger" wasn't his name, I reminded myself, keeping my breath steady and my eyes on the cheap light fixture in the ceiling. His name was George Huggins.

I knew because I'd seen his mug shot. In the photo, his eyes were warm; familiar; friendly, even. His goatee was trim, his expression pensive.

I knew a lot about Huggins now, and what had happened after that night he pinned me to the sidewalk with his gun. His dramatic citizen's arrest had been all over the news back in July. He was charged with the murder of Jinghong Kang in downtown Oakland, a Virginia man in town for a job interview with Google. Kang's death had been a big black mark on the Bay Area's new dot-com boom, the family man shot over a few bucks. Then there was the funny detail of the woman he was with, who was left mysteriously unharmed.

There was another couple, the paper reported, that the police suspected Huggins had mugged after us and before

Kang—a man and woman sitting in a parked car, not far from where I'd been thrown to the cement that night. The man was shot, but lived. Again, the woman was unharmed.

Parker called me at work when the *Chronicle* published his picture. I pulled it up on my screen for confirmation, but I'd known as soon as she said *It's him* that the Kang case we'd been hearing about and our guy were connected.

It was spooky to see him again, those blank eyes, watching. "Laborer," the DOJ database said, under his "occupation." Initial reports suggested he lived out of his car.

I turned on the tap, brushed my teeth in the moldy motel bathroom, careful to look at myself only briefly, warding off the weird energy, the warble between the shape in my mind and the one in the mirror.

"Men," Mom had said. I'd thought that was all I needed to know.

You'd have to be pretty destroyed to hold a gun to another person's face and shoot it, I thought. And you'd have to have abandoned yourself to the core to want to annihilate a child.

I lay in bed and tried to sleep, but I could hear things in the dark, even over the grinding noise of the air conditioner: sirens, creatures swooping across the sky and dive-bombing the highway. There were animals under the water somewhere, moving steadily toward their prey.

I wouldn't sleep tonight, and if I did I would drift in and out of the harrowing dreams that kept my body dazed with exhaustion back home. I'd made a kind of peace with the buzz of it.

I put my hands behind my head, listened to the air conditioner crank, and let myself think about Roy. The last time I'd seen him, back when I was in college, he'd seemed more husk than man, hobbled and graying in a golf shirt and saggy khaki pants. I hadn't been afraid of him exactly, but of what he could conjure.

A few months ago, I'd started a tattoo on my chest that began: *Love your.* It was supposed to say, *Love your ghosts,* but I'd stopped the tattooist short. I wasn't so sure I could commit to that, and now the space above my heart was fill-in-the-blank.

Men, I thought, uneasily. I understood why my mom made that word a volcano, but I didn't know how to situate the bearded man in my dreams against it. My limbs got heavy just as the light slatted through the plastic blinds, and I fell asleep thinking about how I needed to know my father in order to understand his undoing. And I needed to face the biggest ghost of all: How could I be sure there wasn't something terrible and destroyed lurking inside of me?

14

Oakland

June 2010 • 29 years old

Before I left for South Carolina, I'd wake each morning to a film of grief permeating everything: it was in our cereal and our bed, on our pillows and blurring the views from our windows. Parker's rules had grown numerous: no downtown restaurants, no night walking. We'd bought a hatchback to ferry us door to door, but even that couldn't make her feel safe.

I had learned growing up that there's no easy place when the world's teeth are showing, and I'd think of that as I watched her fight back tears—unable to push the car door open to walk 10 feet to a nice restaurant in the concluding moments of dusk—her face twisted in wounded, horrible rage.

"I've been mugged too," a friend shrugged over peppermint tea one day, on the sidewalk outside the coffee shop on Piedmont Avenue, the sun still safely backlighting us, "That's living in the city, right?"

No.

Like a dumbstruck animal, I was stuck on the gun's hover, the back-and-forth skitter of our man, the way his dead eyes had popped when he'd heard my voice. I tried to explain the simmer of his frustration, the way it built and built and then deflated, mysteriously, when he saw who he'd captured. The parts of me I'd deemed dangerous: my female-ness, or at least my not-man-ness—they were the parts that had saved me.

Parker didn't get it. "It's the best thing that's ever happened to me," I said once, and I could see I'd made a mistake by the flash in her eyes, the way she flinched.

She'd say it later, often, to signify our difference. "The *best thing that ever happened to you*?" Her baby brother had died when she was four, so she never loved anything without feeling the weight of its loss. The gun, that ugly reminder, was a symbol of what could happen to my body, what it's like to be left behind.

"The *best thing that ever happened to you*?" The way she said it, it sounded like "*Men*."

A betrayal.

◆

Where I grew up in western Pennsylvania, deer were hunted to keep the population down. Still, we'd put out salt licks and watch whole families wander by. I found I could open the door and approach them as long as I moved slowly enough. They'd lock eyes with me, ears pricked, stuck, as if stopped by time.

I'd get closer and closer—five yards, four, three. I'd reach a hand out greedily and, like magic, their eyes would pop open a little, their bodies hunching into themselves; then, always, they'd spring awake and bound away: big and graceful, alive.

There was an invisible line, a wire I'd trip, and it was

different each time: four yards, two. Every body has a different threshold, but we all know to run eventually; most people don't realize that.

We never forget how to escape.

15

South Carolina

August 2010 • 29 years old

I awoke to the shuddering rumble of a 16-wheeler and took a deep breath of dry air before rising, shirtless, from my bed. My scars grooved into my skin, wide as a thumb under my armpits, narrowing as they made twin half circles across my ribs.

I ran my finger along the raised lines where the sutures once were, charting their fade. After the drains and bandages had come off, after I put on a T-shirt for the first time and felt it hang, correct, on my frame, I'd told Parker that it was as far as I wanted to go, that I was happy to blur between bodies—not male, not female, not quite.

But.

I pushed open the blinds to reveal the dumpsters and semis in the parking lot outside. I felt better in the sunlight. I mapped out my day: a visit to the state archives to research Roy's family, and then a dinner with my uncle that I got nervous just thinking about. We hadn't seen each other in 20 years. I could hear Parker's voice, her easy encouragement. *You got this*, she'd tell me, like she used to.

Say it.

"I got this," I told myself.

I washed my face and combed my hair, focusing on my eyes and letting the edges of my face blur.

Stay, my body warned, so I concentrated on the woodchip smell of my deodorant, the citrus of my cologne. I could project a perimeter of fitted white T-shirts and tattoos, hair gel and minty toothpaste, and if I did it just right I could squint and see the right shape of myself.

I squared my shoulders, marched past the front desk with my cap curled down at the corners.

"Have a good day, sir!" someone called after me, an invisible man, a man who never existed, a man who'd been here all along.

◆

In town, I got a coffee at a café full of beards and tattoos, and even still a middle-age lady glared at me as I poured cream into my cup. I wished Parker was there to bring some levity, to make a joke about hee-haws and how they should be worried about their mom jeans and not her handsome boyfriend.

I loved it when she called me that.

When I was 15, my first girlfriend and I took the bus to the mall and made out in the dressing room at the Gap while a jock high school kid cluelessly handed me jeans over the dressing room door. "You're so much cuter than he is," she'd whispered hotly in my ear, back when I could look in a dressing room mirror and see someone familiar.

"You're like a boy," she'd said, biting my neck, "but better."

I took a deep breath and left for the car, cup in hand. The main square around the University of South Carolina wasn't so bad: your average cluster-fuck of take-out joints, bars, American Apparel. Train whistles were far away and infrequent enough to be charming, and the school itself, sprawling grandly over the sprinkler-soaked green, was picturesque.

Somewhere, some early-partying frat boy gamely howled, "Go Cocks!" Coeds wore the word stamped on their asses, young men in dirty white hats with its double-meaning were all over town, hooting after them. It was hard to imagine my father here, books in hand and a full head of hair, a girl on his arm.

I turned left and found a crew of rough-looking guys gathered around a trash can. I barely dodged the sorriest-looking of them all, who reached out for me with frightening speed as I arced around him, aiming for the gas station across the road, my fist balled at my side.

"Hey," he whispered hoarsely.

The square was empty, the students at class or in the already-open bars, I guessed. I tried to quiet the panic, this new PTSD, so different in quality than the quiet buzz I'd grown used to. This was a hurricane, fast and wild.

I could hear Parker: "Run. Better to look stupid than be dead."

"Hey!" he croaked again, his teeth yellow, his skin leathery.

Despite the prickle of panic, something in me understood he was harmless, old, broken. Anyway, I could always take off. I took a breath, turned around.

"Yeah?"

"Spare a dollar, ma'am? I mean sir?" he asked, and I shook my head no, to all of it.

In the gas station, I leaned against a cold drink case.

"Be careful," Parker had said before I left, which meant not to assume I could handle gangs of men in the semi-rural

South. I had to walk back by the group on my way to the car, and as I passed them I imagined my father. I could see myself land a perfect upper-cut, the snap of his neck, a satisfying, murderous sound.

The men glanced my way, then away again, then hollered at a woman passing by who shooed them off with her hand.

I was safe. The acid tinge of fear in my mouth dissipated and I was left with a terrible, tender grief. I found my way back to the car, and when I finally shut the door the silence was heavy as snow.

I closed my eyes and saw Dad on his knees, Huggins hovering above him on that cracked sidewalk.

Huggins, the gun, my father, cowering: "Run," Huggins whispered. My father rose, escaped.

Maybe my father had spent his childhood saving wounded birds, his college years defending friends in fistfights, because why not? If I was here, anything was possible. Maybe there was some way he could make sense to me.

Maybe, somehow, I could find a way to be my father's son.

16

Boston

January 2003 • 21 years old

The call came on a soggy New Year's Day my senior year in college. My stomach was post-whiskey queasy, my mind dull with lack of sleep.

"I have something to tell you about Roy," Mom said, getting right to it. She only called him by his first name to me, so I, in turn, reflexively insisted on "Dad." He was more than what he'd done to me, he was my father, too.

"It's serious," she went on, and I couldn't help it; I imagined his funeral, how benevolent I'd be. I would say wise things to his grave and my girlfriend would take me home, and that home would actually feel like a real home and not this shitty apartment with the mattress on the floor.

"Yeah?" I asked, trying to be cool.

"Are you up?" Mom switched to her business voice. "This is important."

I roused myself, put out my cigarette in a chipped thrift-store ashtray. I ran a hand through my hair, as if she could see my sorry state.

"Yeah, I was studying."

"Alright," she sounded doubtful. "I don't really know how to say this, so I'm just going to come right out with it." Her tone had that vulnerability that made me antsy, anxious. "Roy was over last night, visiting the kids, and we got into a fight."

I didn't breathe. Once, when I was in high school, I'd seen them speaking quietly, heads close together, in the hallway by the front door. They'd been separated for years, ever since she'd discovered the abuse, but when he'd reached for her hand, she'd let him take it.

"Remember my ex-husband Rick?"

"I mean, yeah, of course." She'd said the marriage ended badly, a betrayal. Drugs? My memory was hazy even on my best days, protecting me with brawny overreach, like an overzealous bouncer.

"Well, he wasn't the best guy in the world," she said, in summary.

"Right."

"But I never told you that when you were two, he sued for visitation," she said. "And lost, obviously. He failed a paternity test."

I lay back on the bed. "Why would he want to see me?"

"Well, I don't know exactly."

We were quiet, until I realized she meant to leave it there. "There must've been a reason."

"He and I were separated when you were born. I didn't have the best taste in men, as you know."

"Hmm," I was noncommittal, not wanting to go down that road. Instead, I drank the stale water by my bed for something to do, and waited.

"I was dating Roy casually, but I have no doubt he's your father. Rick knew about it, and I guess he got spiteful when I asked for a divorce." I studied the bright snow outside my window, hiding its bitter, neck-freezing wetness in a pillow of unsullied white.

"So Rick's definitely not my dad?"

"Definitely not," she said.

"And Roy is?"

"I never doubted it."

"Alright," I agreed.

She lingered too long, and I waited, sensing a wallop.

"The thing is—Roy is your father. But back in the '80s, the tests weren't so great. And when we were fighting, Ellie and Scott heard him say—" She blew her nose efficiently. "I just don't know why he's doing this," she said to herself.

"What do you mean?"

"Roy's test came back inconclusive," she said. Then, quickly, "Ninety-five percent negative."

"Negative or inconclusive?"

"You looked just like him as a baby," she said. "I'm just telling you because he's suddenly forgotten that he's the one who wanted to never mention this."

I couldn't focus. I didn't really want to know. I wanted to wake up again and stretch out all my kinks, to pretend that my life was as simple as the granola in the cabinet and the hangover thundering through me. Beyond my bedroom door, my passive-aggressive housemate, Amanda, washed dishes with pointed clatter, mad I'd skipped doing them again the night before. It was comforting to think of her annoyance, of the snow melting outside, of anything, frankly, but this.

"Why didn't you tell me before?" I asked, hating the timidity in my voice.

"Because what does it matter? He can't weasel out of it 10 years later. He's your father, he did what he did, end of story."

"It matters to me," I mumbled.

"Why? Would it make what he did to you any better?"

"No."

I thought about the model engine, how he skulked around with stupid, watery eyes. I lit another cigarette. The dark smudges on the white blinds suddenly disgusted me. I forgot I was holding the phone until I heard her sniffle, and I fended off a wave of tenderness. I knew the exact redness of her eyes, the startled way she looked when she cried, like she couldn't believe her own sadness.

"So who's my dad, if it's not Roy?"

"It is Roy," she said.

Amanda had quit banging around the kitchen, and the world was so still I felt the snow's heaviness on the roof. The blinds were thick with something. What was that, ash? How many years had the accumulated detritus of bodies dusted this room?

"If it wasn't Roy—" I said dully.

"I had a one-night stand before Roy and I were together. I don't know how to reach him. He was a stranger."

I took a long pull of my cigarette, tapped the ash off until the ember burned clear and bright. Through the screen, the icicles hanging over the sill struck me as dangerous, a foot long each, sharp at the tips.

"Do you know his name?"

"Jim," she said. "Nelson. He lived in New York, we met at a conference. He's not your father, and it was 20 years ago."

I allowed just a moment for a different life, a father who took me on roller coasters and taught me how to change the oil in my car, who suffered a private but perceivable hurt when his parents died, when he felt powerless, when he realized there were terrible truths beyond his control. I watched that imaginary father grow old and die, watched him soften into a body yielding itself to fate, listened to his whispered deathbed chatter, heard how much he wanted me to understand, as he did, that the world could be beautiful anyway.

"I'm sorry, honey." She was, I knew.

"If Roy's not my dad, all the better."

"But he probably is," she reminded me.

"But he probably is," I repeated. "If he isn't, though, great."

"I thought you'd feel that way."

I puffed on my cigarette and concentrated on the night ahead, the Irish bar I'd stop by later, after the blinds were clean.

"I love you, you know."

"I know, Mom." I crushed the filter against the ceramic face of the ugly ashtray. The ember glowed until I pushed the butt hard against it.

Vanquished was the word, I thought. I vanquished it.

He was my father, I decided. Otherwise, he'd never loved me. Maybe, in fact, he'd hated me and my Slavic face, my narrowness, my body a constant reminder—and that was too painful to think about without disappearing again.

It occurred to me, troublingly, that I'd become the sort of person who listened only for the stories I wanted to hear.

"I don't want you to think badly of me," she sounded small.

"I don't," I said, because I didn't.

We got off the phone and I sat for a long time, watching the foot-long icicle drip like an IV in the sun. Something about it made me angry, the way it took up so much of my view, the fact that I had no say over its sharp body.

Amanda said through the door, "I'd really appreciate if you'd do communal dishes sometimes."

I imagined my parents standing so close, I imagined Roy was my dad and then, again, that he wasn't. I imagined hitting him, over and over, until he cried crocodile tears.

"I just feel like we've talked about this a few times at this point," Amanda continued. "It's really important to me to live with people who respect the rules of the house."

I walked over to that old, busted window and opened it as wide as a scream before slamming it closed again. The rattle shook the whole floor, but wouldn't you know it?

That fucking icicle refused to break.

17

South Carolina

August 2010 • 29 years old

The archive's walls were lined with a baffling mix of registries and records, books bound in musty red and worn brown leather. I picked up a few, paged though Civil War ledgers, then put them back down, struck by an otherworldly sense that the books were props in a play about my life.

I tried not to imagine my Uncle John giving me a long, assessing look before allowing me into his house. He and Holly were Southern Baptists, so devout Mom had warned me not to visit on a Sunday unless I planned on accompanying them to church. I tried not to think about him and Holly and how they'd interpret my androgyny or my questions, my sudden appearance on their doorstep, my lack of explanation.

Stay, I told my body.

Okay. Where to start? The sum total of what I knew about my father was sad, but not exactly sinister: his oldest brother had shot himself, and his family had lost their farm in the Depression.

Perhaps more revelatory: when I was young, Mom found a formal portrait of Roy as a toddler, dressed up in girl's clothes. His cheeks were painted pink, his dress ruffled.

There was something of myself in that photograph, though I didn't know how to explain it then. I knew that the boy I saw in the mirror was a template I could put over my body like the transparencies my teachers used with the overhead projector. I knew I needed to do some arithmetic to accommodate him, soften some lines, smudge us into one recognizable silhouette. I knew after college, as the boys around me became men, that I could no longer move invisibly among them; they'd filled out, grown puffy with drink and stress.

The boy in the mirror turned out not to be a passing construction but a vital organ, now missing. If I'm being honest, I'd tell you I was in South Carolina to begin to bring him home.

◆

"What you want are census records, over there," the librarian said, pointing at a huge wooden cabinet. Her blush was smeared visibly, too high on her cheeks. "You can view them in the microfiche machine."

"Okay," I waited for further instructions.

"You've never used a microfiche machine?"

I shook my head, wondering if my voice had already tipped her. Shame spread thickly from my chest to my neck, clotting my throat.

"Let me set you up, honey," she said, her accent like a birdsong. "Come on." She collected microfiche tape like she was shopping for produce, examining each one with an expert's assessing eye.

"Here are the marriage records," she said, growing enthusiastic. "You'll want to cross-check the census ones against these." She tapped them affectionately against the counter. "Alright, son," she said, "let's see if we can load these up then." I kept my head down, a flush inexplicably spreading up my neck, the frightening, lovely feeling of being seen, the discomforting sense of its fragility, the way I was not myself, not at all.

She led me to a behemoth of a box that looked like something the director of an '80s movie about time travel might dream up.

"So, just looking to learn a little about your family?" she asked, threading the tape.

"Mm-hm," I said, low as I could.

I saw what she saw: a young guy in an Oakland A's cap; quiet, searching.

"Alright," she said, flipping the switch that illuminated the census record on the screen. "1920."

I was inexplicably touched by the looping script of the census, the tender care taken by the writer.

"I'll leave you to it," she said. "I'm over there if you need me." She pointed to where I'd found her. Something maternal in her look made me miss my mom, and I fought off a sharp stab of guilt.

Sometimes, our stories are all we have, I reminded myself, returning to the machine.

Exactly.

◆

I mapped my father's bloodline on notebook paper—the things I could see, like when the farm was sold in the Great Depression—and then the pieces I could only imagine: the cotton fields, donkey carts, gas lanterns. I found my grandparents, and their parents, too. I went past the time when the census taker wrote "cannot read or write" next to all the women's names, back when families lived together in strange groups: uncles and grandparents and grandchildren. I found a great-uncle who'd fought for the Confederacy in the Civil War, my blood tainted with slavery in ways I couldn't imagine and didn't want to.

My blood. Or was it?

Did it matter? I'd left that question unanswered back in that last semester of college, and hadn't picked it up since. I was too busy making a life outside of what had happened to me. I was in San Francisco, land of redwood hikes and gay bars, focusing on being a person who wasn't defined by trauma. I'd made "normal" my North Star, and my father didn't factor into my new, better self, so neither did my ancestry.

But staring at the messy family tree I'd just drawn, a blank space where my name should go, I realized I'd been wrong. The answer was a paradox: fundamental and unimportant. Biology wouldn't erase my scars, and it didn't cause them. Whoever's child I am, my body belongs to me.

18

South Carolina

August 2010 • 29 years old

The weeping willows hung low like they do in songs about the South.

I sat in my rental across the street from Uncle John's modest, well-kept Colonial, considering calling him to say I'd never left California. Before I could chicken out, my phone lit up with his home phone number. I answered it before I could change my mind, and found his wife, Holly, on the other end.

"You lost, honey?" her voice sugary and lilting.

"No, ma'am," I answered. "Just pulling in now."

I saw just then that Holly, stout and smiley, was on the front porch, catching me in my lie. She waved as I smiled stiffly and unfolded myself from the sedan, keeping my gait small as I crossed the lawn, trying to pass as someone not passing as a man.

She gave me a quick once-over and pulled me in for a hug. "It's so good to see you," she said in that warm and impenetrable Southern way.

John appeared behind her. They were roughly the same size and shape, like two pears, and I was relieved that he bore only a small resemblance to my father.

As far as I knew, no one had told them about the abuse—Mom hadn't, and Roy wouldn't—but they hadn't seen me in over a decade and who knows what story they told themselves as to why. I couldn't help but wonder if Roy was an outlier, a man gone haywire. Maybe that was the scariest possibility of all.

John surprised me by reaching out his hand instead of going for a hug, a subtle acknowledgement of my masculinity. "It's been too long."

I shook it and agreed.

His eyes were a little rheumy, his hair wispy across his forehead, but the rascally glint in them reminded me of Roy at his happiest.

"Your daddy know you're here?"

"No," I said. "We're not so much in touch."

Holly's smile grew a little tighter, but otherwise we just stood in our small circle, frozen on the front stoop. I felt dumb for tipping my hand so soon.

"Well, that's too bad," John said, finally. "You hungry?"

◆

On our way to the restaurant I pressed my forehead to the window in the backseat. Something about the early-dinner hour and the stop where I was asked to admire their one-room, white clapboard Baptist church gave me a mournful feeling. We sat in the parking lot, both of them gazing at it like God might appear any minute, and their awe depressed me. Maybe it was the energy between them—a sadness I couldn't put my finger on that pulsed in strange waves under their musical accents.

"You go to church, honey?" Holly asked as we got on the road. I didn't know what to say, so I just said yes.

John drove slowly and without the radio, and I found

myself sleepy in the backseat, the sun beating down and the windows open. Our conversation drifted lazily, comfortably, along the river of safer subjects: college football, the muggy weather.

"Are you writing a family history?" John asked, after I mentioned I'd spent the day in the archives.

"No, not exactly."

"You're a writer, aren't you?"

"I am," I said, and we left it at that. You could make an argument, just then, that I was the villain of the story, showing up in their town with murky intentions.

But I wasn't writing a family history; that was true. Our stories intersect and some of them entwine, but I couldn't be responsible for any but my own.

We were quiet until we arrived back at the square where I'd faced off with the group of guys that morning. The greenery of the college struck me again, as if we were rolling through an admissions brochure.

"Roy and I would come here every weekend by mule to go shopping in the markets," John said.

"By mule?"

"Yep, after the Depression," John seemed to enjoy my surprise, and I couldn't tell if he was pulling my leg. His gaze in the rearview made me a little uneasy, but I didn't mean to transpose my father onto his smooth grace, his wink.

"How far was it?"

"Oh, about 20 miles," he said breezily. "We were just kids, then. It was a good time."

"You're serious?"

"As a heart attack."

I knew my father had grown up poor, that one of his earliest points of pride as a young man had been when he'd saved enough money to get his teeth fixed. I knew that his family had been wiped out by the Depression—but somehow the mule threw it over the edge. Maybe his rage was located in somewhere along that hooved path to town, the other kids passing him in their cars. Before I could ask anything else, though, we'd arrived.

They'd picked a restaurant in town called California Dreaming in honor of my visit, an upscale steak joint in a former railroad depot. As we pulled in, I thought about how I could picture dreaming of California there. I'd probably dream of nothing else.

John and Holly were treated with great ceremony at the dimly lit wood-and-brass reception desk. "We come here a lot," John winked, and I nodded. It looked, ironically like an East Coast gentlemen's club. I guessed that here, when they dreamed of California, they saw New York instead.

They sat us at a too-big table in the back. After we ordered, John turned to me expectantly, and I realized it was time to get down to business, though his manners prevented him from asking me why I was there.

"I researched a little about your family at the archives today," I said, self-conscious about the truth revealed by my choice of pronoun. John didn't seem to notice. "They were from Germany?"

"Yes indeed," John said, settling into his seat, "they came over with their own money, in fact. Got a land grant to settle here."

I thought of the mule, the tenant farming. I imagined a fall from grace, an Icarus-like shame that was passed down from generation to generation until Roy, electric with it, discharged it all on me.

"They must have been pretty well-off, then."

"They were, I suppose. But by the time your daddy and I were coming up, we'd lost everything. A man in town bought our house but let us stay on in it, paying rent and watching over his farm." He took a huge gulp of his soda, his tongue lolling a little. Holly drank daintily from her water, squeezing her lemon after each sip as if seasoning it. She was quiet, but watchful, and I couldn't shake the sense of being studied.

A ponytailed waitress came by. "Chicken fingers," John announced as she set his plate down. He looked like a little kid, and it struck me, again, how I could never see the child in Roy. It's like he'd never been one.

I pawed at my fries, trying to think of how to ask more about what I wanted to know: that picture of Roy in the dress, the death of their brother, Tim.

What broke Roy so much that he wanted to break me?

How naïve to think that to pinpoint the cause would scrub the dark plague crowding my heart.

"You get myopic," Parker always said. "Get out of your head."

I looked at John and got the same chill that ran through me whenever I got close to the bone of a larger truth, like when I overheard a stranger at the bar tell his friend that you teach people how to treat you.

I'd been writing my own story all along.

Solving the mystery of who my father was and why he did what he did might make the narrative coherent, but the bearded, shirtless man running through my dreams was most definitely me—and he was waiting, as I'd been on my knees on the sidewalk, to be released.

◆

John looked at me blankly, and I realized it was my turn to speak.

"What were your parents like?" I said, finally. "I don't really know anything about them."

"Oh, good Christian people," he said, cutting up the chicken. "Daddy worked himself to death. You know," he looked philosophical as he set down his knife. "I mean, he really did. Roy's told you that he found him? Daddy was on the floor, half freezing, having a stroke. Roy took him to the hospital."

"He did?"

John looked surprised, then recovered. Holly avoided my eyes.

"Well, yeah. And he died in the hospital."

For a long moment the only sound was forks on plates, then the chatter of USC undergrads and their parents making a welcome racket in the background.

"I'm sorry," I said.

"That's alright. It was a long time ago. Anyway, then Roy graduated college and high-tailed it out of here."

"Why'd he do that?"

"I don't know. Got a good job, came home the day after his graduation and said he was moving, and that was that."

"Do you mind if I take notes?" I asked, and he nodded, on a roll.

"Another thing about Roy," he said, "was when our mama died and we got around to dividing out her things, all he wanted was the shotgun." He shook his head. "Your daddy did love hunting, but still."

I remembered sitting in front of the stone fireplace

in our house and staring at the gun mounted above it, its gleaming wood and long, dark barrel.

I saw Huggins, his arm shaky, the handgun so close I could look into the barrel, dark as death.

"I remember that gun."

"Yes sir, that's the only thing he took."

That bird feeling, a flutter in my chest.

"What was he like, as a kid?"

"Let's see," John said, and I had the spooky sense we were both talking about somebody who'd died. "He was always off by himself in the woods. Liked the peace of it, I guess." He seemed unconvinced, but he laughed. "I was out with girls most of the time."

"Did you all see a lot of him after he went to college?"

"He came over for our weekly dinners when he was at USC," Holly finally spoke, dabbing her mouth with her napkin. "We used to invite the whole family to come by on Sundays, and your father would come pretty regularly." She gathered her silverware onto her plate. "But, of course, he wouldn't be in our wedding."

There was an uncomfortable pause.

"It's true," John said, chewing on his straw. "My brother Tim was my best man, but Roy wouldn't be in the wedding party. He came, though, sat right in the front row." He shook his head, as if warding off the memory. "Strangest thing, though."

"Hmm," I kind of coughed.

"I guess he doesn't like talking too much about himself," he said, making it sound like a joke.

"I guess not."

They waited, but I left it there.

"Come back home with us," he said, paying in cash,

waving away my card. His eyes were a warm liquid brown like my father's and my siblings', but without the lace of green that spun through mine. "I want to show you something."

◆

It was cool in their house, a nice contrast to the syrupy air outside. I tried to focus on that and not my intense desire to leave as John rooted around upstairs. Holly and I sat in their all-beige living room, looking at endless pictures of their grandkids.

"Here it is!" John said, clutching the handrail and looking suddenly very weak. He hobbled down the stairs and handed me a hardcover genealogy book that some cousin had put together for a family reunion. "Everything you ever wanted to know about the Lewises, right here."

It was strange to see Roy's last name embossed across a book, the name that had been mashed against my own, a hyphenate, until my mom took me to the social security office and they unceremoniously lopped it off.

The story was worthy of the leather cover: the great-great-grandparents that were maybe mine, on a ship bound from Germany, sea-whipped and salty. The land grant, the Manifest Destiny, the years of cotton and then the Great Depression and the poultry farm and railroad café they ran themselves, working from daybreak to sundown. There were dozens of great-aunts and nephews and cousins, so many of them, a whole family that might belong to me.

I imagined visiting John and Holly every year, drinking iced tea in the back yard, shooting the shit about who's an alcoholic and who's getting a divorce. Holly brought me another photo album and a glass of water.

"You're in this one," she said, pointing to an archaic, glossy 4x6. I looked five or so, smiling like a champ in front of their perfect front door. Roy's hair was almost black, and my mother beamed a bright, toothy grin. My siblings and I stood dutifully alongside our cousins, this mysterious family with their religion and their accents and their carpet that sagged in spots and smelled like potpourri.

And I knew, looking at that picture, that I couldn't fail the kid in it any longer. That kid had that haunted look of a child keeping a secret bigger than their body, those dark circles under the eyes, that far-off gaze, otherworldly.

I could see it plainly in Ellie, Scott and Roy, and then looking up at John: Roy was not my father. I looked scrappy and dark, and they were fair and tall, round a little in the face.

This journey couldn't end here, I realized, and even though I'd known it all along, I got that chill again.

"You cold, dear?" Holly looked at me carefully, and for just a minute I got the sense that she knew exactly what I'd been thinking.

"I'm good, thanks," I tried to turn my attention to John, who'd been telling a story.

"He was named for Roy," he said, "who was the most important man in town."

"Oh yeah?" I didn't mention that my dad had often said he hated his name—another of the handful of things I knew about him.

"Now, our uncle was a strange guy," John said, adding, more charitably, "A real character."

Two lamps and the stairway light pooled feebly, leaving the rest of the house dim. Holly got up and switched on the kitchen light and a few extra lamps. I could tell that they didn't want me to leave and I felt lonelier than I had since I was a kid. It was a claustrophobic, wet feeling. I remembered: lying on my bed in damp clothes after getting caught in the rain on the way back from the bus stop; Mom and Dad in their separate corners like prizefighters, he marooned in the basement and she in their old bedroom. I didn't want to strip naked, didn't want to be alone. I poured myself a bath, locked that big bathroom door, and later when Mom knocked, I pretended I couldn't hear her, just to get that worried timbre to rise, high in her throat.

Stay, I told my body.

"So what was the deal with the original Roy?"

John leaned back in what was clearly his special chair—a mustard-colored, puffy thing. "He owned half of Swansea, but did he look like a vagabond! He had a wild, long beard and a stink like you wouldn't believe." He whooped kind of like Roy did, a good ol' boy sound. I shifted uncomfortably.

"Once, Uncle Roy bought a Model T in straight cash. He may have smelled to high heaven but nobody pushed him around."

I tried to appear charmed.

"He took a special interest in your father, what with our parents naming him for him. He brought him bars of candy and made special trips to see him. Once he brought him a silver dollar, a real one."

Alarm rang through me, straight into that sore spot in my heart reserved for the saddest of things. "So did Uncle Roy spend a lot of time with my dad?" I asked, but John deflected me, asked Holly to fetch a tea from the kitchen. I looked at him, his big, stiff body aimed politely toward me.

John leaned in, as if anticipating my line of questioning.

"It's so good to see you," he said. "It's funny how fast life goes. Don't forget." He wiped his rheumy eyes.

Holly came back, bearing tea. "Excuse me," I said, and hustled to their bathroom.

I shut the door and soaped my hands with a seashell bar, trying to gather my thoughts. Roy, a young Roy, had probably looked a lot like my brother. I could juxtapose and adjust their faces and then, there he was: little Roy, handed off to some creep in a Model-T.

Like me, I let myself think, and my heart spasmed until there were fireworks in my chest, the pressure lifting.

◆

"Got to get up early tomorrow, got more research. . . ." I trailed off, after I joined them back in the living room.

"Well," John said, struggling to push himself out of his chair. I averted my eyes, but he noticed. "Your daddy has arthritis too," he said.

"You're in touch?" I tried to hide my surprise, but Roy's refusal to engage with his family, even minimally, was part of why I was here, why I was so sure he had something to hide.

"Well yeah," he said, "more recently. He came down to visit last year." He gave me a look. "I'll be sure to let him know you were here."

"Alright," I said, a part of me glad at the idea. Let him know I could go anywhere I pleased, that I couldn't be locked in or out of rooms any longer. "Thanks for dinner, and for making time to catch up. It means a lot to me."

"You're family," Holly said. She led me to the door, letting John get himself up. It was clear we weren't supposed to help. "You come by anytime you want."

She pointed silently to the bedroom as we passed, a metallic, beastly machine next to the bed.

"What's that?"

"He got diagnosed with prostate cancer last year," she said quietly.

"Is he okay?"

"It's been a rough patch, honey," she said, and I worried she might cry. Maybe that's why he and Roy were back in touch: a close call, a hospital stay. I wanted Roy to be decent. I could see his tired smile, building us a tree house. I could imagine him finding his father paralyzed by stroke, and carrying him over his shoulder.

"I've got it beat now, though, don't you worry," John appeared behind us.

"I'm glad to hear it," I said. He looked sick, come to think of it, withered, like a man caving in on himself.

"Come back soon, okay?" he asked.

"I'd like to," I said, surprised to find that I meant it.

"Time flies," he said again, shaking his head. "You just never know."

I gave him a hug this time, with an extra squeeze, because he was right, but I'm sure we both knew I'd never see him again.

◆

On the drive back to the hotel I thought about Roy and his mule, his special hunting gun, his dying dad. I could see him, a little, like a memory coming alive, and it didn't matter if I was right about his story or not, only that I gave him the human shape of one.

I switched to a country station and listened to the raw,

nasal anthems about heartbreak and wicked women and their version of what makes a man. I learned the choruses quick enough to sing along, even though I didn't particularly like it, just to see what kind of person I'd be if I were someone else altogether.

19

South Carolina

August 2010 • 29 years old

The road out of Columbia was mostly empty the next morning. John had offered to show me the old farmhouse in Swansea, but I wanted to go somewhere I could be quiet with myself, far from the COCKS hats and the hunters, and mostly away from John's familiar, sad eyes.

It was a beautiful, bright day, even if the landscape was dotted with weedy concrete strip malls, litter, unkempt lots of double-wides. The hot rain started up near the strip club and stopped at the town line, just in time for me to kick up real red dust on actual dirt back roads. There was a beauty to the devastation, the dilapidated white plantation house, the hawks circling the bare fields.

I drove for miles, making a picture with my mind of the rain clouds and pastures, the wooden fences and the road signs. When the sky cleared, I pulled over and watched the cars go by, trying to figure out how to best say goodbye to Roy. I knew that he wasn't my father—in some animal way, I could smell in the thick air the lifetimes and bloodlines that had nothing to do with me.

Of course, I needed to know for sure. But a paternity test meant contacting the old man, and we hadn't spoken in 10 years.

One pick-up passed, then two, then a beater with an

American flag on the antenna. I tried to imagine growing up on a landlocked farm, far from a city or port, my family my whole world. I closed my eyes, leaning on the car, breathing in the corner of the world that—in one way or another—had shaped me.

There wasn't a lot to see, and I had one more stop, anyway: the Baptist cemetery deeper into the backwater where John had said my grandparents were buried. It took me some time to find the tiny church, which looked almost bleached in the midday sun. A guy mowing the field across from the plots gave me a quick salute, both of us sweaty in the thick heat, and I nodded back, a man for all the world.

I found a dozen Lewises: decades and decades of stillborn babies, victims of flu, cousins removed and removed again.

I looked around to confirm that I was still alone. "Hi, Grandma," I said, surprised to find myself moved by her headstone. I touched the letters of my grandfather's name: L-E-E. "Grandpa."

We were all together just then, our stories overlaid, even Roy's. I was right to come here. If you want a sense of the real architecture of a person, go to the place that grew him, visit the family—my family, I corrected myself.

Because Mom was right, in some ways it didn't matter. What mattered was that I could stand in the same place he'd once stood. That's another law of physics: nothing created, nothing destroyed. We just come back, again and again, and see the deer and hear the creek and taste the ice-cold soda on the back porch.

If I couldn't be erased, then neither could my past; if I was going to change form, like so many rambling houses sliding off their foundations, then I wanted my structure to be honest so that it could be sound.

20

California

September 2010 • 29 years old

Back home in Oakland, I ran.

I ran to the summit of Piedmont cemetery and watched the lights of the Bay Bridge twinkle through the fog. I ran down to Lake Merritt and past the courthouse that housed George Huggins's pretrial hearings every month—I knew, because I followed the case closely. But the more I ran the farther away I felt from the clarity of that night in April. I was running away from something else.

My body knew. My body led me to my laptop late into the night where, illuminated by the monitor's sickly light, I read about the effects of testosterone: lower voice, facial hair, easier muscle gain, redistributed fat. I watched endless videos of guys a decade younger than me, injecting a one-inch needle into their thighs.

Risks included liver problems, cancer, diabetes.

Relationships.

I closed the laptop, put it away. I ran loops and more loops. I looked for myself in the burn of my calves, the gasp of my lungs.

"It's not a choice," trans men on YouTube said, over and over. "I was born in the wrong body."

Truth isn't binary, though. Everything, in the end, is a choice.

Still, I got it. I was compelled, carried by a force as strong as the one that propelled my legs down 41st Street, away from Huggins. It was the same drive that pointed me to South Carolina, it was what kept my heart open, despite all the reasons I knew to seal it tight against the world. There is a great beauty in what we know but can't explain. You can call it faith; I do.

◆

"You have to fight for yourself," Parker had said when we first got together, and again, and again. "Wherever you are," she'd said, "whoever you are, you have a right to be here."

21

California

September 2010 • 29 years old

When we got engaged many months ago, a wedding had seemed the perfect opportunity to dress up like adults, and somehow magically become them. But that hope felt strange and wrong now, silly even. Now we avoided writing our vows, though we powered through the rest of the checklist: we ordered the sparkling wine and flowers, briefed the friends who offered to DJ, to make our rings, to cater.

"The ceremony," I said, finally, tired.

"Everything changes," Parker answered, a disappointment and a fact we'd stared square in the face. What could we promise, knowing that anything was possible?

It was my sister who showed us. Ellie was to be our officiate, and in the weeks before the wedding, she pivoted into spiritual counsel. She'd written a thesis on Tibetan sky burials, she worked in a hospice, and then with people living with HIV. She knew about impermanence, and suggested we might not fight it.

"If we're going to get married," Parker said to us both, "I don't want to talk about 'forever.' I want to talk about right now. I want to respect you, and you to respect me, and for us to agree to be ourselves first."

"Looks like you have your vows right there," Ellie said.

"We do," we answered, in that kind of chorus that only comes from years of synchronized speech. It had become easy, in the tense months since I'd begun running, that we'd always already agreed. Everything else was ceremony.

◆

I looked through the eucalyptus trees the morning of our wedding, the sliding door of our cabin open and facing the water. Mendocino was warm as an East Coast summer day, and the grounds hummed with our family and friends, pitching in. They directed cars to the ceremony, took photographs, prepped food and moved chairs and knocked on the door to ask if there was anything else they could do.

"What if I change a lot?" I asked.

"Then you change a lot."

I'd been knotting my tie, but I lay back on the bed, and Parker lay down beside me. My buttonholes matched her dress, and it felt good to be suited up that way, like a team. I held her hand, thought of the rings my brother had in his pocket. "ROOTS" was engraved on the inside of hers; mine said, "OCEAN."

"How do I know we'll stay together?" I asked, and she looked at me like I knew better, which I did.

"We don't," she said.

This was our new beginning, along a windy spot above the wild Pacific, everyone gathered in a jagged, imperfect circle around us. Later, I'd come to think that this moment was made all the more exquisite by that night in Oakland, when we learned we could be both powerful and fragile at once. Love isn't a promise—it's a truth as uncontained as waves and as unmoving as the redwood groves we drove through, holding hands across the gearshift the whole winding way back home.

22 Oakland

November 2010 • 29 years old

When I told my therapist about the feeling of running, the spaciousness in my chest, the soreness that surfaced in its wake, South Carolina, the testosterone research, Huggins's monthly hearings, the paternity test, the unfinished business of what makes a man, he smiled at his own insight.

"Maybe it's not the running away from Huggins that changed you," he said. "Maybe the question you should be asking yourself is 'What am I running to?' "

I shrugged, annoyed at the implication, knowing he was right. His office was in a drafty Noe Valley Victorian, and I held a wilted paper cup full of bitter peppermint tea and tried to "be in my body."

"Where are you right now?" he asked, and I tried to feel into my blood vessels, the muscle in my jaw, the thick skin on the soles of my feet. "Where do you feel yourself?"

I knew that we are hormones: stress and sex. When we're attacked, when we freeze, when we can't land a punch, we become cryogenic in our fear. When we see a man in the mirror but the man's not there, we stop, not wanting to upset the senseless universe, the one that holds us still.

"My knees," I said, feeling in them a wavy constellation of power and fear, remembering the cold fog in my throat, the sickly light from the TVs shining through windows as I ran and ran, the electricity and possibility and terror pumping through my jackhammering legs.

My survival was in my muscle, a stink of adrenaline that had trailed me all the way down 41st Street. My survival was curled in my fists, atrophied in my biceps. My survival was not a faraway memory, but a live and animal part of me kept dormant, a snarl I'd mistaken as harmful, an instinct in need of release, an energy that couldn't be destroyed, only ever transformed.

◆

"So," I said to Parker as the nights grew long.

She poured a little whiskey into the chili. "Sew buttons." She laughed at her own joke.

"I really am thinking about taking testosterone."

"I know." She went back to stirring, dismissing me.

"I'm more serious than before." We'd had this conversation probably a dozen times.

"Okay."

"If I were to, actually, would you still want to be with me?" I tried not to sound as scared as I felt. I wasn't sure exactly what hinged on her answer anymore. "I mean, you would, right?"

"I think so." She seemed nervous, perhaps sensing the shift in my tone. Her ambivalence gave me a hitch in my throat. I must have looked deflated because she turned the flame down, opened the fridge, poured us two glasses of wine, and sat down. She clinked her glass to mine.

"To being yourself," she said.

"To being yourself," I told her.

"Now," she said. "I like you how you are, so I don't want you to change."

"I want to be with you, though."

"I know," she said. "And it will probably be fine."

"You sound unconvinced." I felt far away.

She sighed. "Let me see you." She made a motion with her hand like *twirl*. "I'm imagining."

I turned around slowly.

"Yeah, you'd look the same," she said.

"That's it?"

"Okay, here are my feelings." She got that warm, sad look in her eyes, and I could see the effort she was making. "I'm really nervous that you'll be different. I'm afraid I won't be attracted to you. What if we fall apart just as we're getting started?"

"Nothing's wrong with change," I said defensively, the truth in her fears a dissonant note to my story, even if I knew she was right. I watched her move liquidly back to the chili, her body a whole that functioned together, not like my collection of jangly parts.

"Let's cross that bridge when we come to it," she said, over her shoulder. "Is this something you really need to do right now? Why don't you think about it more?"

I followed her into the kitchen. "I feel—"

"You're going to figure out the right thing to do, okay?" she said. "I believe in you, I really do."

Before I could stop it, I was in the grip of huge, racking sobs. Parker put her arms around me and held me close enough that I could hear her rabbit heart. After some time, I lifted my head from her wet shirt.

"I have an idea." She disappeared into the bathroom and returned with a bottle of mascara.

"Look at me," she said. She turned my chin gently, dabbing a smeary approximation of scruff on my face. She sat back with the brush head between her teeth, examining me.

"I could get used to this," she said.

I didn't want to leave the moment to check the bathroom mirror, so I pulled out my phone and took a picture: me in the foreground, Parker with her head on my shoulder.

In the dim light and without a flash, the shadows and my white thermal and blue fisherman's cap combined, their magic making me into the man I envisioned, the boy all grown up. I looked right.

"Wow," I whispered, my hand shaking, and continued to stare.

"Hey, Narcissus!" Parker said, and I blushed and put the phone down.

"You think I'd be a good man?" I asked, once we'd eaten the chili and put our feet up.

She didn't hesitate. "Do you think you're a good person now?"

"I do," I said.

"Well, then," she answered, as if it were obvious.

III Fight

23

Oakland

November 2010 • 29 years old

The Rene C. Davidson courthouse is a harsh, functional stone building. I could see Lake Merritt from its windows, and I looked outside as I waited in line, wondering how many attorneys with stained ties and tired-looking administrators had seen me jog around its light-strung path.

"I'm looking for information on an inmate," I said to the annoyed woman behind thick glass in braids and a business-lady suit.

"I can't tell you much, just the next court date," she said, not meeting my eyes.

I knew where to look up Huggins's information, knew that he was scheduled to appear later in the month. I'm not sure what else I thought she'd know—how to contact him, maybe, or when the depositions and delays might end and his trial actually start. My messy pompadour and lunch-break dress shoes put me at odds with the oversize fur-lined parkas and Disney sweatshirts in line behind me, and my difference embarrassed me.

When she asked for his name and the date he was arrested, I gave it. When she asked for his social, I saw she thought we were connected, and I briefly imagined Roy in prison, saw him in some barren visitor's room, waiting for someone, maybe me.

"Oh!" she said to her computer. Her booth was full of pictures of a child with braces alongside phrases like "Inhale the future, exhale the past." I imagined being boxed up all day in the low light, talking to miserable grandparents and brokenhearted mothers, and felt touched. She leaned closer to me and whispered with a sweetness she'd been hiding all along, "In for a 187?"

Her look was thick with sympathy. *Murder*.

"Yes," I said.

She explained the coding on the next deposition hearing. "It's about evidence," she said. "Probably whether or not to include something."

"Do you know when the trial will start?"

"You'd have to ask the lawyer," she said. "I wish I could do more."

I thanked her, turning back toward the crowd of grandmothers.

"I'd come to the next hearing," the woman called after me. "It'll be winter recess soon, so you probably won't have the chance again for a while."

The families watched me curiously, the only white person among them. This flawed country, this broken system, all of us crowded into this hot room with our sad stories.

I could feel the uneasy pain, the collective worry taking root in my own stomach. Maybe the key was finding our overlaps, I thought, as a young guy in a do-rag nodded at me. I nodded back, passing as the person I wanted to be: a good guy, someone who wasn't out for revenge but for something brighter.

24

Pittsburgh

October 1998 • 17 years old

Sometimes Dad would come through town to see Ellie and Scott, a complicated arrangement that made us all uncomfortable, but especially me, and not for the reasons I suspected my family thought.

I never had the guts to say that I wanted him to drive me somewhere symbolic like the meadow across the bridge where we all went to get stoned after school. You could watch the planes take off from there, you could pretend you were anyone else. I wanted him to say, "I wasn't always this kind of man." I wanted a coded allegory, to learn to tie a lure, to get into a fistfight with him and break his front tooth, then to smoke a cigarette and have the whole thing finally be over.

Instead, he would nod at me and I would nod back, then go upstairs, smoke a contraband cigarette flagrantly in my bedroom, pack a weekend bag.

"Hey," he said one October day, catching me on my way to call my best friend to see if he'd give me a ride downtown. Otherwise I'd take the bus, the long stretch of Ohio River Boulevard. I'd listen to my headphones, count smokestacks, imagine bigger, prettier cities.

"Come on, I've got something to show you," he said,

shrugging on his tan work jacket. I tried to remember the last time we'd spoken past a pleasantry.

Our bodies had changed since his fingers held my thighs in place. His hair was more silver, his movements stiffer with age. I looked so much like a teenage boy that I'd mostly forgotten my difference. It was only at odd moments that I'd pass a mirror and see shapes that shouldn't be there, a stranger who looked like me but wasn't me at all, a stranger like a kick in the chest.

I trailed my father into the hallway, affecting a distant civility but planning my night: call my girlfriend, who lived latchkey in Pittsburgh and whose father, mysteriously, allowed me to stay, without restriction, in her fancy refinished basement bedroom. We'd go to this diner down the street, she'd probably be hot and cold, she'd probably say she was in love with some boy she met last summer. She must have known that only made me like her more.

"I got you something," he said, lacing his boots. I kept my hands in the pockets of a too-light windbreaker, pretending to hate him; also: hating him.

"Cool." The weirdness between us tugged at me.

He opened the door and we were delivered into a woodsy autumn day, where a used maroon Dodge Intrepid sat, boxy and dented, in the driveway.

He smiled like the time he'd come home with that model engine, picked out special for me, and handed me the keys.

"Really?" I asked, and he nodded. For just a moment, it seemed like everything could be different.

Mom opened the door, came out with her arms folded across her chest. The two of them eyeing me made me suddenly tired, the gravel poking into my soles, the leaves decimated by the wheels of a car that wouldn't make up for anything.

I threw my bag in the passenger seat and slid into the driver's side. "Thanks," I said, like it was nothing.

"We were thinking you pay the insurance and for your own gas." He sounded timid, which made me so angry that I blinked away stupid tears.

"Do you like it?" Mom said from the doorway, and I knew that she was giving me the normal life she'd wanted for me, that this is how she loved me.

"Yeah," I said, fiddling with the radio.

"Good," she said. I knew to call out, "Thanks, Mom," to summon up the part of me that saw the gesture for what it was, and meant it.

"Be safe," she said quietly, and shut the front door.

That left Dad and me, a crumpled sort of hope on his face. I pinwheeled through sadness, disgust, and affection until, finally, I flipped the car in reverse, looked back with my arm behind the passenger seat.

"Wait," he said.

This is what I saw in you that reminded me of myself.

There was a long pause. "You should gas it up with premium every once in a while," he said. "I mean, between the cheap stuff. Keeps the engine running smooth." He coughed, patted the car like a dog.

It was the only advice he'd ever give me.

I cranked up the classic rock so I couldn't hear whatever he said next. "See you," I said, tapping a cigarette out of the soft pack and into my mouth, lighting it with my free hand, daring him to act like a father, giving him another chance, wanting, more than anything, for him to say, again, "Wait."

25

Oakland

November 2010 • 29 years old

Winter came on hard. The fog rolled in early, the rain wet through my jeans. I walked home from my job as an employment counselor, work I wasn't qualified or suited for: I worried about my clients constantly, pictured Tanya in the homeless shelter without her daughter; or Lawrence, who'd just been fired from the supermarket and stopped showing up at school. My afternoon was ragged with high school kids in need of laundry detergent, kids who couldn't read or write, kids whose parent wouldn't let them go to college, kids whose fathers were dead, who were about to become fathers themselves.

I walked out of the building, three blocks from where Huggins shot Jinghong Kang, the churchgoer with a degree in physics, the father of three sons. A simple guy, he only owned one suit, his wife told the *Washington Post*. He could fix anything, she said. A man's man. A family man.

I let myself get cold, I shoved my hands deep in my pockets. Stooped old ladies waited for the bus, teenagers in jackets far too heavy for the weather horsed around, shifty guys hobbled by crack didn't notice the misting rain, while guys in fancy Northface jackets kept themselves dry.

I passed them all and thought about Huggins's court date the following week. I wanted to go, but I wasn't sure why. "You're compelled," Parker said in her offhand way. "Go on, then."

I walked past men in hoodies, men in dirty jeans, men in suits, men without teeth, men with perfect teeth. I read that when you take testosterone, you turn on different genes: this one determines how hairy you'll be, this one your muscle mass.

I watched a group of boys shove each other playfully on a sidewalk near an intersection, too close to traffic. They made cars move around them, like little kings, until one kid almost got clipped and they were forced to stop. You could see the way they realized, however briefly, the limits of their bodies.

Men. We're only defined by the boundaries between us. If I was going to find myself, I needed to find Roy.

◆

It was easier than I expected. A Google search led me to Thompson Construction in Bend, Oregon, which listed him on their site as a vice president. I didn't doubt it was the same Roy Lewis—he'd been in the construction business since I was a kid. Teachers used to ask me what I wanted to be when I grew up and I'd say a mechanical engineer.

I studied the site copy. "Precision, trust, efficiency," it said.

Parker made herself a cocktail and then watched me from the kitchen doorway, her whole body backlit, a silhouette in light. In the last blast of the setting sun, her hair was so blond it was nearly white, like a ghost or an angel.

"You look like an angel," I said, and I couldn't make out her expression even with a squint, but I knew she smiled, despite herself.

"Come on. Whatcha doin'?"

"I'm writing to Roy," I said in my best casual voice. I knew I looked rumpled, my hair a little wild. She turned on the lights ahead of the coming dark, then returned to the doorway and studied me with impressive nonchalance. "Alright."

I sat uneasily in front of the blank email. I wanted to know if Parker believed, deep down, that men could be good. I also knew, in that language-less way I'd known to go to South Carolina, that I couldn't ask.

"So," I joked instead, "what would you say is the best greeting for a child molester?"

She laughed without much feeling. "I say go for the gold: did you abuse me because I'm female? I think I'm a man but I can't figure out how much you have to do with it."

I looked at her dumbly. "You know about that?"

She put down her drink. "You're not subtle."

"Do you think he hated women?" I didn't even know the theory existed until I found myself saying it. "And because he hated women, I hated myself?"

There it was, the freeze, like the moment before Huggins told me to run, before I learned that what I needed to shift the story was in this body all along.

"Hey," she said, coming toward me, the sass drained from her tone. "Your gender's been the same always, okay? It's not something that's done to you, it's who you are."

"I know."

She leaned down and wrapped her arm around me, leaning her head on my shoulder, her breath a little boozy on my cheek. "But if you were willing to believe that, we wouldn't be talking about it."

"What would I do without you?"

She shrugged and sat down at the table beside me. "Probably you'd be pretty much the same."

"I don't think so."

She smiled, and I knew we were both right. "How about 'Hello, would you take a paternity test?' "

A shimmer of grief ran the length of me. I thought of my client, the kid who was about to be a dad, how happy he was that the baby was a girl.

"Hello, Roy," I wrote, not calling him *Dad,* not wanting to insist on it anymore; even if it somehow turned out that he was my blood, I wasn't going to lie and claim him as my father any longer.

26

Oakland

November 2010 • 29 years old

The bailiff held us in a dank vestibule outside the courtroom on the third floor. His crew cut and big, squishy face gave him a jockish, upbeat quality that annoyed me, but everyone else shifted back and forth and stared blankly in his direction, tolerating his condescension, waiting for him to move. "Don't make hand gestures at the inmates," he said. "Don't try to communicate with them in any way."

He scanned our faces. "They know you're here for them," he said, almost tenderly, and then, finally, swung open the door.

The prisoners were lined up behind a short wooden divide, on a platform, shackled at the legs; a dozen guys, slouching in their cheerful, Easter-egg-colored jumpsuits. We sat in wooden pew-like benches, heavy with initials and messages that people had carved, somehow, under the bailiff's watch.

Free Tish

R + L always

The windows ran with condensation under laboring heaters, and the room had the terrible, edgy energy of primal grief. I tried to focus on the inmates and not the couple beside me, who looked mournful and hollowed out.

They say there are two primary story lines: a stranger

comes to town, and a man goes on a journey. I thought about that night at Uncle John's, how then and now an argument could be made that I was the stranger, the potential villain. I thought about my client whose cousin had just been shot downtown. For all I knew, the shooter could be the kid leaning back on his chair in front of us, pretending not to be scared despite his baby fat and quivering lip.

Parker and I had called the tip line once we'd seen Huggins's mug shot on the news, but I knew—with a sudden, flooding relief—that I couldn't send anyone to prison. Justice looked a lot like revenge to me. I imagined Roy doing sit-ups on a cement floor beside an open toilet, and for the first time I found that I was glad to not have opted for retribution back when I was 10 and given the choice.

As we waited for the judge, I recognized Althea Housley—George Huggins's girlfriend and suspected accomplice. She hadn't been present at our mugging, but I couldn't help but wonder if she had been the source of my reprieve, the inspiration behind whatever logic Huggins used to let me live. She looked bedraggled and deeply sad in her weirdly cheery pastels. I'd seen the grainy security footage of them walking briskly away from the spot where Kang lay dying in downtown Oakland, her face clear and his hidden under that Vader hood.

Housley's beaten-down demeanor had me back when they'd both been all over the news, and it was surprising now that she looked exactly the same in person—hunched over, heavy in the mouth. She stood out among the nameless grizzled guys, that teenager grinning self-consciously into the courtroom, and George Huggins, who I finally recognized.

Without his oversize hood, he was much smaller than I remembered. 5'10", according to the arrest record, and 190 pounds. "He's tall, really tall," I'd told the officer that night, "enormous." In truth, he was only a little bigger than me. I imagined fighting him, landing a body blow that crippled him, then sending a nice right hook into his stubbly jaw.

He looked dead ahead, ignoring the whispers of his lawyer, who'd shimmied alongside him to talk in his ear. I waited for him to notice me and when he didn't, I stared at the enormous American flag slung over the courtroom wall, counting the stars and trying to breathe deeply into my stomach.

Panic curled the corners of my vision as my heart grew loud and painful, like it meant to escape—with or without me.

Stay. I brought myself back to look at Huggins again: my ghost, just a man. He met my eyes and we were the deer and the hunter, though I wasn't sure who was who, only that I felt pinned, again, by his gaze, my heart clattering, my head cottony, the squeaks and coughs and murmurs all isolated and subdivided, until the room seemed alive in a way it hadn't just moments before and we didn't move. I didn't want to; I didn't want to look away.

27
Pittsburgh

1990 • 10 years old

Not long after the police chief came, I crawled on top of the covers next to my mom during one of her lie-downs. I was too old to do such a thing, but dusk brought on a seasick feeling, the memory of whatever had happened during those lost hours never entirely gone but not exactly present, an amnesia that made me feel crazy, erased.

"Mom?" I asked, and she put her arm around me and pulled me close. We were quiet for some time, and I wondered eventually if she'd fallen asleep.

"Your golden core's right in your center," she said, suddenly, turning over to touch my heart. "Can you feel it?"

I stared at her. She smelled like minty toothpaste, her hair tickling my forehead.

"You are perfect at your center. Okay? Nobody can ever touch it, and nobody can take it away from you."

The spot she pointed to felt like a cold drip, like water slicking the wall of a cave. It did not feel golden, but I was afraid to say so.

"Never forget," she said. "Promise?"

I nodded, listening to her heartbeat, to the gurgle in her stomach. She pushed on my sternum as if marking the spot, and I pressed my own bone, felt the pressure release. It was a sweet sort of pain.

I pushed against the tender place again, hoping.

"Okay?"

I knew she was afraid. I could feel the buzz of her anxiety every time she'd come to bail me out of the vice principal's office, never really punishing me for talking back or acting out, which only ever made me feel worse.

She rubbed my back as despair sloshed around in my stomach. On one hand, I knew that there was something mysterious in me; an opening right where she'd pointed, infinite in its space for homeless old men and weeping moms, a softness that felt innate, a self apart.

On the other hand, I worried I'd been infected, like an animal with rabies. I worried I'd wake up dead-eyed, whatever he'd planted in me ready to strike.

"Okay," I said, but not because I meant it.

"Golden," she said again, her voice strong and clear, as if she could sense the argument I'd have with myself for the next 20 years, as if she knew that there would be a time when I realized it was all, finally, a matter of perspective.

28

Oakland

November 2010 • 29 years old

I held my breath and watched Huggins watch me, my body drifting up and up, as before. *Run,* I thought, but no, I would not leave. The running catapulted me right into this moment and I didn't have to be still or disappear anymore.

Someone sniffed, someone else shifted squeakily in their seat, a clatter of change fell behind me.

Stay.

I came into the fabric of my shirt, tight against my chest; then a chill along my neck; then the damp of my armpits. I came into my right lid's nervous twitch, the hunch of my shoulders, the press of my toes in my shoes: all of it proof that I lived.

With a whoosh, sounds returned to my ears with their blurry din. My breath grew steady as I focused on Huggins's jaw, the chestnut of his eyes, the off-white glow of his teeth. I could see myself pressing my fingers into his neck, and yet I was sure that his body was just as worthy of love as my own. I was sure that he and Roy were no different from me; not because we were monsters but because we all have the chance to be more than the worst that's done to us.

If you tore the roof off the courthouse, if you went up and up at lightning speed, we'd disappear. Maybe that's heaven, you know? It seemed possible to me, in the dry heat of that courtroom, that heaven was a metaphor for the grace of perspective you get when you die.

"Court is now in session," the bailiff announced, and his voice disconnected our stare. "Please rise," he said; and I thought of church as we, as one, did.

29

Oakland

January 2011 • 29 years old

At work, Ronnie, the new dad, came back in to say that his girlfriend had moved down South, and she'd taken the baby. He showed up with sleep in his eyes and the worn look of somebody who'd been drinking and not much else. He'd lost his job, he said, the one I helped him get at a big box store in Emeryville.

"What should I do, Miss?" I tried not to flinch. How was he to know that the assault of language grew worse by the day, that the word made me waver like a hologram? How was he to know that I lay in bed every night abuzz with the strange sense that my body had a plan for me that even my mind didn't know?

Ronnie wasn't the father, or I was beginning to suspect he wasn't, anyway. His file said he was developmentally disabled, which I knew didn't mean anything for sure: many of my clients got stuck in Special Ed because they'd never been taught to read. But I'd helped Ronnie with enough online job applications and mock interviews to get a sense of his confusion and his gullibility. He'd be easy to manipulate, and the story he'd come in with over the past few months seemed all wrong: she cheated on him, she didn't want to see him, she'd told people the baby wasn't his. He shared each piece of it with the same stunned, slow cadence, his eyes wet with disbelief.

"She broke up with me for good," he said. "She told me Erika wasn't my concern. Why would she say that?"

"Can you get visitation?"

He shook his head.

"Ronnie," I tried, carefully. "Are you sure that she's yours?"

He looked so surprised, so unsure, that I wished I could take it back. I knew better than anyone that the answer to that question was intimate and complicated, that it didn't matter and yet it mattered more than anything.

"Yeah," he said, finally. "But she won't take a blood test, which the courts say I need. And now she's gone."

I murmured reassurances that we both knew weren't true. "I just want to send some diaper money," he said, wiping his face on his shirtsleeve.

"That I can help you with," I told him. I knew that Sears was hiring, and maybe Home Depot, too. "You're a great father," I said.

He smiled at me finally, this great, toothy smile. Then we got to work, because he was going to be a dad whether he was a dad or not.

◆

After Ronnie left, I sat at my desk for a long time.

Even though Roy and I had sent in our mouth swabs the month before, the testing company hadn't yet contacted me with the results. I'd told myself I was too busy to follow up. Parker and I were preparing to move back East, and our lives were consumed by both the fantasy of our future and the logistics of planning for it, arranging for airline tickets, moving trucks, yard sales.

But, if I'm honest, I hadn't really wanted to know. Something about living the between-ness of our situation felt right: he was eternally my father but also forever maybe not. It gave me, strangely, a sense of possibility, as if he could be redeemed by the answer.

"Abandon all hope," I'd written on a Post-it note, and I watched it move gently beneath the heat duct. I read it in some book. The idea was that hope misses the point: it's either going to happen or not. You can't make a new reality, only fashion something real from the one that you've got.

◆

I fiddled with the phone cord until the frazzled receptionist returned to the line. She'd been gone long enough to make me consider hanging up several times, but I couldn't, not with Ronnie having just been in this office, willing to show up to whatever his life delivered him.

"Looks like—" she said hesitantly, and I knew right then. I tried to reach out and grab the last moment like an errant football, like my dad and me playing catch. The final time I'd think: *my dad*.

"We have ruled out the man tested as a possible father."

A long suck of time passed in which the spray of gravel, the model engine, and the knobby-handed grab coalesced and I understood. "Okay."

I looked out my window, at the little-sister skyscrapers of downtown. A few blocks away, surveillance cameras had captured Huggins stalking like death toward the 19th Street train station.

She said she'd send me an official letter, but I'd have to go to a facility in person if I needed to be tested for legal purposes. I thought, crazed just for a moment, that maybe Roy had asked someone else to swab a cheek in his stead.

"How accurate are the results?" I asked finally, possibly interrupting her rambling directives.

"Ninety-nine point ninety-nine percent," she said with clear pride. Then transitioned, awkwardly, into a tone of sympathy. "Can I help you with anything else?"

It's so random, when you think about it: who dies, who gets born.

No, I told her. That's all I need.

◆

The office was empty. I could see people down below punching open umbrellas or pulling their hoods into tight circles around their faces. I fought the urge to throw something out the window, to take off running into the weakening light. I struggled into my jacket and took the service elevator down to the street, a magnet pull guiding me past coffee shops and galleries, drugstores and fast food places, immigration law offices, and bail bond and check-cashing joints, until I reached the 19th block of Webster.

It was here, across from the dental office, that Kang, a man who could have been me, bled to death. I studied the sidewalk's texture; I rubbed my fingers along its sandy skin. I looked for bloodstains, I got on my knees among the hardened gum and bottle caps, and stayed there until a child looked out the picture windows of the waiting room and saw me.

I got up, my knees pulsing just a little, and I felt the

sore spot in my chest with my fingers. I could work it like a knot, each push opening a spangle of sadness. I pushed as I walked along the lake, then up past the grocery store, the new condos, the movie theater, the laundromat. I pushed until I felt my body fill with a warm light, mysterious and natural as freedom.

IV Rites

30

Oakland

January 2011 • 29 years old

I learned to lift properly under the guidance of a white-bearded trainer named Mike. He owned a pick-up and a shotgun and I'm relatively certain he didn't think of my gender much at all. He didn't call me "brother," but he didn't "ma'am" me either.

He was gruff, though philosophical. When I told him about the mugging, he said he'd pulled a gun on someone once; some dude who'd tried to carjack him. His knees had gone to jelly facing the other guy's shotgun, despite the 12-gauge in his hand. "It made me feel small," he said, and I wasn't sure if he meant his own gun or the other guy's. Maybe both.

"You feel strong now?" he grinned, watching me deadlift twice my weight. "You're a big shot."

Mike was like a really wild uncle, part survivalist, part musclehead. "Eat protein!" he hollered at me as I left each workout. "An egg a day, and you'll be all muscle."

I'd told him I wanted a broader chest, more bicep, but he focused on my core instead. "Your arm muscles are too long," he said regretfully. "And pecs are really hard to develop when you're not male." He looked away at that, respectfully. "But your core. That's your power, anyway."

He showed me how to throw a punch, a jab from the

shoulder. "Feel that?" he asked, poking my torso in his sweaty gym. We stood in front of a mirror, the light from Rockridge Avenue blaring into the subterranean, moldy space.

I couldn't help but think of my mom, of the soft spot beneath my sternum. I could see her, reading the letter I'd sent her after the paternity test, sipping a scotch and soda to take the edge off, crying in that embarrassed way, even if no one was there to see it. I just want the truth, it said, but I wasn't sure that was true, exactly.

I didn't want her to be sorry; she was always so sorry. I wrote that, too. I wanted to start over. But I worried she wouldn't write back, and the thought that the story she'd told us both for so long might be more important than the truth of who I was becoming clenched me up in anger.

My jaw tightened just thinking about it. "Hey, man, pay attention," Mike ordered.

I pulled my punch, but the jab to Mike's outstretched hand must have stung, because he winced.

"See? All core. Don't let anyone tell you otherwise," he said, before sending me back to do sit-ups next to the punching bag. I watched my face appear in the mirror, rising over the mountain of my legs, alien as moon rock.

I closed my eyes and tried to focus on the ropy pull of my abs tightening into a fortress around me. "First you have to tear the muscle," Mike said. "Then it rebuilds itself even stronger."

I couldn't quit seeing him pulling that shotgun out from behind the headrest of the pick-up. He'd thought he might shit himself, he said, but he'd held the gun level at the man reaching into his open window, then he'd peeled out of that parking lot before the other guy could react.

"I probably shouldn't have pulled the gun," he said, reflectively. It was an ongoing conversation now, weeks after he'd first told me the story. He stood above me, spotting while I bench-pressed a pretty meager 40 pounds. I don't know what got him on the topic; maybe just a sensitivity to our size difference. He had six inches and 150 pounds on me. "But I lived. No shame in that."

I thought of how it felt to freeze under Roy's hand, under Huggins's gun. I thought of what I knew I needed, deep in the growing core of me.

"It's not fear that kills you in that type of situation," he said. "It's what you do with it."

31

Tulum, Mexico

February 2011 • 30 years old

In her stripes and sunglasses on the plane, Parker looked glamorous in a way that had me wishing I'd dressed up a little. "Let's go to the ruins, and the beach, and the little town tomorrow," she'd said. Then, "Or, okay, just the beach." She leaned back, distracted by the view out her window. "Look at the water," she ordered, and we watched the delicate blue of the Gulf below.

"You're like a tornado," I said, a refrain, and she laughed.

I didn't tell her the degree to which I'd agonized over my swimsuit, the straw man for bigger anxieties; the way my late-night testosterone research had reached a sort of furtive apex. Then there was Roy, writing back that he'd be happy to meet me before we set off on our move east. I could leave Oakland, drive north to Oregon, then leave the West Coast behind. "I'll answer any questions you have," he wrote.

We'll see about that, I thought. Some questions live in a lost part of you, they beat hard against whatever you construct to hold them.

I tried to read the in-flight magazine and not think about Roy or my chest. The two felt connected, like I couldn't allow my body to masculinize without confronting him in real life. In the meantime, the twin man in the mirror was growing more solid while my current, softer face became more and more transparent. I knew which body was a ghost.

Parker smiled at me, her eyetooth cute and jagged. I knew I'd have to tell her, and that even if she said she'd stay with me she couldn't know, not really. Not any more than I did.

So we had another round of G&Ts and watched the water crinkle and glitter beneath us, and I tried to think of nothing but this moment, perfect and suspended and held above it all.

◆

"You're married?" the clerk asked. He smirked, his face boyish and a little mean around the lips. I gave him a hard look.

"Yes," Parker answered, polite and warning all at once.

"Okay," he said, "just making sure." He handed me the keys with ceremony bordering on the sarcastic. "So this is your honeymoon?"

"Yeah," I said. "Is this the first time anyone's honeymooned here or something?"

He closed his mouth and pressed his lips together. Later, he handed us margaritas and set us up on the beach to bat idly at mosquitoes and listen to a mariachi band. We ignored his tittering with the waiters as we walked past, his *Buenas noches, señoritas*, thick with the international tang of cruelty.

Despite him, Parker and I spent the week lounging on the beach enjoying the fancy resort. The gay men in banana hammocks paid us no mind, and I could wear a shirt or not. On my birthday, we went scuba diving in an underwater cave full of waving coral. We'd both almost chickened out, panicked by the sensation of breathing under water, the mechanical click and hiss of our masks.

"We have to do this," I told Parker, and we did.

"Come on," our instructor said, after we practiced and panicked and practiced some more. He turned and left us to decide whether or not to follow him, past the baby barracudas and the clownfish, the sunlight in beams you could swim through, our air pressurized but delicate, our bodies fragile yet buoyed by each and every one of our animal cells.

Afterwards we watched a cadre of gulls feeding across from our cabana. They dive-bombed the waves and reappeared with fish, like miracles in their beaks. We rented a scooter and raced through swarms of mosquitoes, the stars clear and hard above us.

I lay in our bed under the thatched roof and tried to imagine nothing changing, but I couldn't picture it.

My body doesn't have a future, I realized. The thought felt heady and airless, like when the space shuttle detaches from its boosters and all of us, watching from Earth, find ourselves left behind with nothing but prayer.

◆

In the water, late in the week, I tried to ward off the mournful feeling of vacation's end. My chest pinkened so I flipped off my back, raising my head up and out of the swooshing, soundless water. Parker was ashore, watching two Americans with baseball hats and zinc noses and ill-fitting swimsuits set up alongside her. I could tell from her upright back that she was nervous at how they'd react to me, shirtless. I understood, too, that she would always be afraid for me and my foreign body; on beaches, in emergency rooms, in backcountry bathrooms.

Back when we moved to Oakland, they'd found a trans woman dumped on an exit ramp off the freeway, just left there on the shoulder like a used mattress or an old couch. I drove past the spot regularly enough that I found myself worrying over her body, wishing I knew where it had ended up.

Then there was Brandon Teena—the trans man raped and killed in Nebraska by his girlfriend's brother and his friends, back when I was in high school. He hung like specter, another man that could have been me.

Parker shielded her eyes to look for me, and I considered staying in the water for hours, turning into a prune until the Americans disappeared. I told myself the couple looked harmless, they'd be curious or maybe rude at worst.

I thought of Mike saying it's not the fear, it's how you react. I'd been reading about manhood rites, rituals almost always related to war: piercings, tattoos, feats of bravery. Then there were vision quests, adulthood as spiritual connection. No matter the culture, you had the separation phase—where the boy walks alone; the liminal time—when he is neither man or boy, but between; and the reconnection—when he returns to his community and is recognized as a new man.

Fuck it, I thought. I stood up in the thigh-high water and began to walk the distance to shore. The tourists stared at me, slack-jawed. I walked until I couldn't stand it, until I half-swam, half-crawled through shallower and shallower water. I rolled ashore, chest-to-sand like a beached whale.

I watched Parker as she gathered a towel to bring to me, and I knew there wouldn't be a divine intervention, no right time, no sign that testosterone would make me a good man, no test to confirm that I would be happier, or more whole.

"You okay?" she asked, above me, wrapping me like a burrito. "I'm sorry."

"I'm sorry," I said, pulling the towel tight. I knew I might have to go it alone, but nobody would bring me to my knees again.

◆

At the Cancún airport we watched thick-necked college guys drinking overpriced plastic-cup beer at the Jimmy Buffett bar. A woman with frosted fingernails stood sentinel outside the women's room, and her curious look spooked me. I sat at the gate across from her and waited her out, removing my ball cap then putting it back on. A linebacker-size boyfriend emerged from the men's room, and they took off, but when I stood at the crossroads between the two entrances, I couldn't decide what to do.

"I can't do this," I told Parker, back at the gate. She put down a Graham Greene book she'd found in the cabana closet. She was grumpy, tired, not interested in returning to Oakland after this reprieve from loud sounds and shrubby shadows.

"You can't do what?"

I sat down beside her. "I'm going to transition. I mean, I think I have to."

She raised an eyebrow. "You just decided that now?"

"I'm serious, Parker." I feared she'd say that she hadn't agreed to this, not really; that the face she married was part of the promise I'd made her.

"Wait, you really mean it this time?"

"Yeah."

She frowned, just a little, but I saw it. She started to speak, stopped. I could see that I'd hurtled us both into that liminal space, and that she'd have to make a choice, too.

"If you mean it, we'll make it work."

I tried not to imagine her secret thoughts. "*You have to let people love you,*" my therapist always said. "*What are you running to?*"

In that moment the ugly airport bar blasted another round of "Margaritaville." We laughed a little too hard.

"So?" I asked, the word trailing.

"Honestly, I'm freaked out," she said. "But if I was going to leave you over this reveal, I never knew you at all."

"Thank you." I tried not to look as emotional as I felt.

"Look, let's get a margarita. I think we need a drink. Personally, I need a Jimmy Buffett souvenir cup. No vacation is complete without a tchotchke and a gender transition."

"I know you wanted to have a different life," I said, not wanting her to joke it away.

"My life's mine," she said, serious now. "And yours is yours."

I knew she was right, but it was still unsettling.

"So you can't really promise me anything," I asked, not really asking.

"That's kind of the point, remember?" She quoted our wedding vows. "I'll never get in the way of you being you. But I can't promise you anything else."

I felt like I was watching that space ship detaching. No, I felt like the astronaut out in space, holding a thumb over the Earth and everyone on it. If it's true that there are only two kinds of stories, then it must be equally true that sometimes you're the hero and the stranger, both.

A drunken series of whoops rang out from the Buffett bar.

"Thank you," I told Parker. "This was really graceful of you."

"Good," she said, looking away from me, and I knew she was probably blinking back tears. "So let's go get those fucking cups."

32

Oakland

April 2011 • 30 years old

The one-year anniversary of the mugging came and went as I got to the strange business of picking out a new name. I narrated my life in third person, often in the rearview mirror. Somehow it felt safer to experiment with assuming a new identity while in transit. I was James and Adam, Oliver and Paul. *James is on his way to the grocery store, Adam went to grab some boxes, Oliver packed up the books in the bedroom, Paul called the moving company.*

Parker voted Adam, but it felt unfamiliar, disconnected. "The first man—really?" I said, because I didn't know what to do but joke around.

The move came on too quickly, but once a body is in motion it stays in motion. Parker seemed less nervous, anyway, excited to be going somewhere hot enough to eat a popsicle in the summertime, where she could wear shorts without worrying over the fog. She wanted an ocean she could swim in, a place that felt quiet and predictable.

I just wanted to get going, to keep moving, to find my way to a different destination. My skin felt itchy and ill-fitting, my name wrong in my own mouth. I didn't know who I was, just who I wasn't. If I was a stranger to myself, I wanted to be a stranger to everyone else, too.

So we flew out to Providence and signed the lease on

a massive, two-bedroom apartment in one whirlwind visit, and I ignored the free-fall feeling I got every time I tried to envision my life a year out. I just saw bright white, the kind of backlit oblivion they say you experience just before you die.

◆

The facility in Boston that would supervise my transition sent along a checklist: get a physical, a therapist's letter, sign these consent forms. The tasks felt manageable, if endless.

Months had passed since I initially sent my mom the letter asking who my father really was, and she still hadn't responded. I housed a hole in my chest that I worried at even as I tried to ignore it. I'd not contacted her again. It felt necessary: nature abhors a vacuum and so does narrative, but I found a freedom in being out from under a story that no longer worked for me. Her instinct to take charge when I needed her—the bubbly cursive detailing exactly what Roy had done, and even the moment she thought she might kill him—had been a comfort as a kid. If I was going to be my own man, though, I needed it to be my own story without her translation.

I didn't know how she'd feel about Thomas, but as soon as I landed on it, I knew the name belonged to me. I gathered evidence: Thomas meant *twin,* Thomas sounded like glasses and a light beard, Thomas clicked into place and then I couldn't un-hear it: *Thomas isn't here right now, but he'll be right back.*

Thomas was also the name of my late uncle, the only man in my family that I look like. He was sensitive, an artist, different from his raucous and science-minded siblings.

He died of cancer when I was a toddler and he was only in his twenties, not much younger than I was now. Mom loved him fiercely; she was always protective of the black sheep, the underdog. I knew that part of the reason I wanted to be named after him was to bond myself to the blood I knew was mine.

It was a name that made peace. Thomas tied me to history, even the hard parts. Thomas wouldn't forget where he came from; Thomas would be his own twin.

"I'm Thomas," I told Parker, who I'd found in the garden, harvesting strawberries.

"Thomas," she said, and it sounded awkward in her mouth.

Later she told me she practiced, that it was like working a muscle. She had to break it down to build it up again: I was not on hormones, my voice was the same, my body the same, but she already saw me as a stranger: *That's Thomas, my person. Thomas is at work. Thomas loves the forest, and two sugars in his coffee, and me.*

33

Oakland

May 2011 • 30 years old

"I guess this is it," Parker said, not sadly. The apartment was empty but for our air mattress, some clothes and a few dishes, and the television. It looked a little forlorn to me, but she seemed relieved.

I was glad to go, too. After the initial email blast (Subject: Big, Huge Changes), then the follow-up phone calls, the drinks and the stumbling switch to "he," I was tired of the vague discomfort that colored every interaction, every friend afraid to screw up my new name, every horrified reaction to a slipped "she."

I waited on my mother, the feeling stretching like taffy: not exactly tension, not hope. I'd sent her a corny pamphlet: *When Someone You Love Is Transgender*.

I looked around the empty apartment and thought that life couldn't get any more uncertain. Parker must have felt the same, because she got up and opened the windows. "This is depressing," she said, letting the light stream in.

"Thomas," she practiced, I could hear her discomfort in the inflection. "Thom," she corrected, the only person who called me that, sounding more at ease, "I'm excited about the garden, and the space, and the hammock, and the summer, and the beach we can swim in."

It was my turn, but dread pulsed in my chest. "I'm excited about new beginnings," I managed.

"There are no new beginnings," she said. She sounded disappointed.

"I'm sorry," I said. "I just don't know what I'm going to look like. It's kind of terrifying."

"I know."

Despite the emptiness of the apartment, I felt claustrophobic. "Okay," I said, concentrating. My body was my body, it would just evolve. All I had to do was allow it to emerge. "Maybe there aren't new beginnings, but I think this is the closest a person can get," I said, finally. "I'm excited to find out who I am when I look like myself."

"Probably you're just you, but more so."

I knew that's what we were both betting on.

◆

"So we're really driving up to see Roy?" Parker sounded annoyed. We were a few days from take-off, eating burgers at the pub down the street from our house. She stole my pickle, as usual.

"If you're going to be mad at me, you can't eat food off my plate."

She sighed. "I'm not mad, it's just I don't want this whole trip to be about how your dad does something super shitty to you."

"Parker, knock it off."

"I'm sorry, but it's a reasonable concern."

"I don't care what he does, that's not the point," I mumbled, though I knew that if she asked what the point was I wouldn't have the language to explain it.

She knew, too.

"You don't have to come," I dipped my huge fries in ketchup. "You could stay in Portland with Alex and I could come back and pick you up."

"I don't want you to go by yourself," she said.

"It's fine," and it was.

"Are you going to be Thomas when you see him, or not?" she asked.

My stomach clenched. I wiped my face with a napkin. "I have this feeling that I need to thaw." I hadn't told anyone else about the freeze, so I checked to see if she understood. She nodded. "So a part of me feels like I need to show up as Page, just so I can't tell myself later that the only reason I could be present was because I wasn't being the same kid who got hurt."

"You're always going to be that kid," she said, not unkindly. "Even a transition won't change that."

"I know," I told her, but I wasn't sure I really did. Some small part of me still wanted to be normal, to be born again. And yet, there was a child inside me, afraid of men, and I wanted that kid to see that we could meld into one being, that I could be all of my selves at once.

"I don't know if I want to get into the whole trans thing with him," I said, because that was true, too. "And I want him to face me the way I look now, the grown-up version of the kid he hurt. It feels important." My face felt hot.

"Okay," she said. "Thom," she practiced again. "If I'm doing this, I don't want our whole cross-country trip to be about whatever messed-up thing he says, okay? I'm psyched to get out of here, to see this part of the country, to spend time with you where we're not freaking out about—" she waved her arm around, and I understood she meant Huggins, the backfiring motorcycles, the car that couldn't keep us safe.

"I get it, that's fair."

"Do you really get it, though?" She eyed me. "I'm serious."

"Yes," I made a promise with my face. "I don't care if he's an asshole. I'm not scared. I need to get past this."

"You know, it's never that you don't make sense, it's the degree to which I want to follow you."

"Well, to what degree do you?"

"I'm still deciding," she said, in a joking voice that wasn't a joke. "I can't handle one more thing right now." She took long pull of beer. "So we can do this, but I can't make it better for you if it doesn't go how you hoped."

"I can take care of myself, Parker."

"We can both take care of ourselves," she agreed.

"Trust me," I said. I looked at the pictures of boxers on the pub wall behind her, vintage black-and-whites, mustaches waxed, arms posed. I thought of Mike, of the way I'd finally have pecs, of the importance of the core.

"Someday I'll look like this guy," I said, pointing at a dark-haired, thin one with a busted lip. But of course, without knowledge of a father's genetic blueprint, I had no idea what I'd look like. "The great unknown," I said to myself, but Parker seemed to know what I meant.

"You'll look so handsome," she said. Then a bluegrass band kicked up, and we nursed our beers in the darkening bar until it felt like the equilibrium between us readjusted, and then we walked the long way home, past apartments we'd looked at when we'd first moved to the neighborhood so many years before. The moon was full and we kept a deep silence like a pact between us, space enough for what we didn't know.

◆

My mom called in the last days before we headed north to Oregon. I let it go to voicemail as I passed the taco trucks on Broadway on the walk home from my final day of work. Ronnie hadn't been back since he got hired and then fired from an oil-change place in East Oakland, but he texted to say he was doing okay, thinking about going down to Alabama to change the mom's mind. I didn't warn him off, just told him he should do what felt right. "You know what you need to do," I wrote him, because I wished, when I was 19, somebody had said that to me.

Golden core, I thought. Maybe I'd heard it long before I was ready to understand what it meant.

I ducked into a service door near a car detailing place and dialed into my voicemail. "Oh, honey," Mom said, "I got your letter." She had been crying, I could hear it in her scratchy voice. "Of course I love you no matter what."

There were more words, but I couldn't hear them. I sat on a curb on a warm day, 3,000 miles from home, and realized simultaneously that I would have given up my mom if I had to, and that I was profoundly grateful for the person she was, despite the ways she'd sometimes allowed her stories to eclipse my reality.

"I'm working on a letter to you about Roy," Mom said. "I'm going to explain everything."

I thought of umbilical cords and that wintry day so long ago when she told me a different story: the one she needed to be true. I understood why. If he wasn't my father, then his only connection to me was her. She blamed herself.

I took so long to decide to transition because I doubted myself, but Huggins lowered the gun because of this voice, this body. Strange to think of it this way, but how could I not? Perhaps the scars Roy left, and the way they held me hostage, turned out to be exactly what saved my life.

34

Road Trip

May 2011 • 30 years old

The backseat was packed full of our things, and the pushed-forward front seat forced Parker's knees to the dash. Furry Lewis howled some joyful sadness and the crowns of firs lined the ridges of the mountains. We climbed north into cold mountain towns full of fishermen and generations of lumberjacks, pick-ups and shotguns, clean rivers, weed farms.

"What are you going to say?" Parker asked from the passenger seat, her window down. We wound around a rock hill, a forest spread beneath us in soft greens.

"I figure I'll just ask him who he thinks my dad is." I tried to sound confident, but I hadn't thought past seeing him. Seeing him was the point. "It's not like we need to have a big confrontation."

"I'd want to kill him," she said, so quietly I barely heard her.

"Well, I don't. Or I don't right now. I want to face him. I just need to see him as a person, not a monster."

"What if he acts like one?" she asked, sitting up. "A monster, I mean?"

"Then I guess how I choose to see him will be up to me."

"Sounds pretty Jesus-like," she teased.

"I am angry," I said, though my anger felt muffled. "I'm

just more interested in moving on. Sometimes anger makes you miss the point."

"How do you mean?"

"Like with Huggins or Housley—I saw them, and they were just messed-up people, you know? But if I'm mad or scared, I can't see that, and then all these people take up too much space in my mind. But if I see them as human beings, they aren't a threat to me."

"Who are you talking about?"

"I guess everyone: Huggins, Housley, Mom, Roy."

"You're the opposite of him," she said, meaningfully.

"I know."

"You don't know."

"Okay, I don't know. But I believe that something turned him rotten, something terrible, probably the same thing that happened to me. So I can't sit around thinking about good and evil like that."

"It takes up too much space?"

"It does." We watched a hawk glide past the windshield, predatory and sleek. "But I do believe that facing what you're afraid of pretty much guarantees you won't become it."

She nodded, and I knew she both saw my point and didn't exactly agree.

I wished I could lie in the woods like I had as a kid; the air sharp, my boots muddy with life. I put my hand to the aching part of my chest, felt its strange waves.

Parker kicked up the volume on the stereo as we cut deeper into the mountains. She eventually slept, her head lolling around until I nudged her skull tenderly against her seat. I loved the peaceful feeling of her, sleeping, as I watched the last light get squeezed from the sky. I thought about Roy, what I really wanted from him.

Nothing, I realized. Being here really had nothing to do with him.

She woke as we hit flat land again. "Where are we?" she asked blearily.

Around us, miles and miles of cows milled dumbly. We could have been on the way to my grandparents' house in Scranton for all the small farms and country houses.

"Almost there, but we could be anywhere, huh?"

"We chose to be here," she said, closing her eyes. And she was right.

35

Bend, Oregon

May 2011 • 30 years old

"Good luck," Parker said as I closed the door to our '70s-ski-lodge motel room. I looked back at her, parked in front of some nature show on the green-and-yellow bedspread, like I was already gone.

"You got this," she called after me.

On my way out of the parking lot I passed a parade of Little Leaguers running hysterical circles between the cars, boys that couldn't have been more than 12. I saw myself in their gangly, prepubescent bodies, their manic energy, their desperate desire to be known.

I saw their need, their untied cleats and stained white pants, all of the terror that could befall them. Bile rose in me, tainting their figures in the dusky sunset. I could meet Roy at a stupid tea shop in this dumb town and hit him square in the mouth. Nobody would fault me for walking away with bruised knuckles marked by teeth, a trophy.

What makes a man? For so many, it's power cut with grit. I'd seen enough movies, I knew the best way to settle things was a fistfight or a beer. Even if Roy didn't know to call me Thomas, even if he didn't see the man in me, I could speak his language.

The darkness came on fast and I turned the radio up, trusting my mind to decide while I wasn't paying attention.

Instead I thought of Parker, who felt strangely like a wispy memory, as did the warm hardwood floors of our Oakland apartment

I pulled into a parking spot in a strip mall of chain restaurants and left the motor to idle. I could feel my legs as they'd pumped that night in Oakland, the chemicals unleashing in me a desire to do more than survive. I couldn't stay a wind-up doll pushing through each moment, a facsimile of myself.

I couldn't, wouldn't hit Roy. The anger fell away like armor until I was left with the story I'd hidden all along. It whistled through me, my first broken heart: regardless of anything, he was the only father I had.

The dashboard clock hit eight. What makes a man isn't who he isn't, but who he is when no one else is looking. I didn't need a father to teach me that. I just needed to open the door, and see for myself.

◆

A block away from the tea shop we'd agreed on, I spotted the blurry back of a white-haired, balding man in slouchy khakis that I knew, with primal certainty, belonged to my dad.

I knew to think of him as Roy. I had trained his first name into my mind much the same way I had my own, but the physical reality of him—the stooped shoulders, the sagging skin, the wounded bearing of a dying bird of prey—he was my father. The word felt painful, a hockey puck hitting the ragged net in my chest.

Something about the way he lingered outside the shop, looking inside and then back out into the street, pulled at me. I could see how his coming to meet me, not knowing why he'd been summoned, was itself a kind of bravery. Not the medal kind, but the decency kind. I was only a few yards away but he hadn't spotted me, and he looked small and human in his jacket, zipped up against the cold.

I hustled to catch up as he turned to go inside, and found myself behind his liver-spotted crown, catching the door he'd held out blindly for whoever followed him.

"Roy," I said, and watched him stiffen. He turned around, grinning, and offered me his hand.

"Hi, Page," he said tentatively, my old name familiar on his lips, and I thought of twins, I thought: tonight and tonight only, I can be every incarnation of myself.

I took his hand, nubby and liver-spotted and soft as silk. It was the first time we'd touched in 20 years.

◆

"Well, where do you want me to start?" He spoke in an accidental boom. I found his new, tissue-paper skin distracting. We were perched up on barstools, his hands so shaky I worried he'd spill hot water over both of us.

For a moment I saw his head, young and glistening, his eyes looking up at me with dull expectation, as if to signal that he could make my body do anything. Now, spellbound by his silver halo, I could feel myself transported to every movie theater I'd had to leave because a man with a similar crown sat down and threw me into a panic.

Stay. I blew on my peppermint tea, watched the water rear back in the wake of my breath. There were bad café watercolors on the walls, and I studied the foamy rivers and fir tree vistas as though they might lead me back to myself.

Parker wanted to know why I'd come here, and I hadn't been able to tell her, but it was clear to me that I wanted to say goodbye—not just to Roy, but to the person I'd become in response to him, and to the body I'd allowed to hold me, petrified in time.

"After the paternity test, I just wanted to know more," I said, and waited for his response, the lilt of his accent, the big bang of memory colliding with the man before me.

"Well," he said, leaning back. "How about I just begin at the beginning?" He cupped his enormous green tea with his hands, like a child or a very old man.

I waited, but I wasn't terrified, or enraged, or numb. I was watchful, acclimated, present. I was Thomas Page McBee, whether he knew it or not, and all of my parts fell into place.

I nodded my go-ahead, imagining a story, like a machine, clicking into motion.

"In 1979," he said, "I took a job working with your mom in Hickory, North Carolina. I was still married to my first wife, Ann, but our marriage was in trouble, and we lived apart. Your mom and Rick were separated."

I tried to take notes to keep my hands busy, but the table was shaky, giving my handwriting a psychotic, jagged edge. I imagined asking him to hang on as I threw a sugar packet or two underneath the wobbly leg, the two of us working together toward a goal, father and son, and I felt my face color.

"But, your mom was a bit of a flirt," he said, coughing into his palm.

"Jesus," I said. I could feel the vein in my forehead emerge, my fists tightening into threatening balls. "What the fuck?"

He flinched, fiddled with his spoon, its clanks amplified as an oncoming train.

"Look," I said through my teeth. I focused on my feet, the hook of the metal stool, the hot tea in my hands. "I just want to know the stuff about me," I edged my tone with warning. The anger felt good, an electric fence pulsing to life.

A table of teens cackled in unruly waves beside us. I'd spotted them coming in: dirty-cornered textbooks sat largely neglected on the stained tabletops, bitten pencils lay dormant behind their ears.

"Okay." He held up his hands. He looked wounded, like he might blow away. His eyes were this earthy, chocolate brown that I knew he hated ("shit brown" he called them), but they were tinged with hurt, they always had been. "Okay. So we got together in 1980, and she told me she was pregnant a couple of months later. I wanted to be a dad," he said flatly. "In fact, that's why my marriage was dissolving—my wife said she wanted kids, but was doing everything possible to avoid having them."

The words sat like something dead between us. I kept my mouth shut. I'm not the kind of man that destroys something smaller than me.

I'm going to be okay, I realized.

"I was serious about your mom back then. But I don't think she really believed me." He was quiet for a second. "I loved her." He said it as if I might not believe him. "I love her still."

"I know," I said. I thought of them whispering and holding hands in the hallway. I'd defended my scrappy territory halfheartedly after that, always waiting to have to make a choice worse than whether or not to send him to prison: where to go if he ever came back.

But I never had to. Mom never remarried Roy or anyone, never even dated a man again. She lived like a monk in her condo, her grief fused with guilt, the combination its own kind of freeze.

Roy looked imploringly at me, and I remembered his crocodile tears. Maybe they had been real. I'd never had the chance to decide.

I looked at the kids beside us more closely: young, healthy, dabbed with acne. Some were surely hiding cuts on their wrists, drugs in their backpacks, incomprehensible secrets. Roy stirred his tea, his knuckles swollen. I felt stricken with tenderness for all of them, the same feeling I'd had in the courtroom in Oakland.

"I was a jealous guy," he said, a confession. "Want me to keep going?"

I pulled my eyes away from the high school kids, thinking *they have no idea how much they know already*.

"Yeah," I said. "Tell me everything."

◆

"So we were seeing each other and she got pregnant, but we couldn't tell anyone we were together. We were both separated by then, but the company had a strict policy against dating. So your mom had a plan."

"What was it?"

"This is going to sound weird, but once you were born, she and Rick had an arrangement, and it involved acting like you were Rick's kid."

I nodded, thrown.

"We were in a serious relationship," he said, as I

searched for something to say. His voice pitched up an octave. "We saw each other every weekend."

"Yeah," I said, embarrassed for him. "Okay."

"Rick knew you weren't his, it wasn't physically possible. He went along with it for his own reasons, an arrangement they'd made. But it got kind of out of hand. When you were a toddler, you even thought he was your father."

"Did that bother you?" I wasn't sure why I asked, but it was out of my mouth before I could consider it, and the lie of my whole life was suddenly alive between us.

"Your mom wasn't sure about us, didn't know if I'd stick it out with her, and she wanted you to have a dad," he mumbled, as if reciting a bit of propaganda he no longer believed in.

I waited. He looked up at me, and must have understood what I really meant.

He looked at his hands. "Of course it bothered me."

There was no way to know if he was telling the truth, but I wanted so much to believe him.

"So, anyway," he said, "I stuck around, like I said I would, and she told Rick one day that she couldn't keep acting like he was your father."

"Just like that?"

"Well, basically. But I guess he was in some kind of denial about it, because he sued for visitation." He looked angry—protective, even.

Maybe, I realized, Roy had loved me at some point. Maybe he'd come because there was a grief that gripped him, too. I blew on my tea, watched the ripples and imagined that they carried away every story I'd ever told myself.

Some mysteries will never be solved, and for sure he was one of them.

◆

"So," he boomed on. "As part of the proceedings, Rick was asked to take a paternity test. It came back negative, no surprise. I'm not even sure why he went through it, but it was costly for all of us." He shook his head. "Your mom asked me to get tested, too, for my own peace of mind, I think."

"I can still remember the results coming in, how she said, 'I have something to tell you.' She was crying, in great distress." He stared at his tea like it would finish the story for him. "That was the worst day of my life."

I gave him an *Are you fucking kidding me?* look, my hand so tight on the cup I imagined the shatter.

"The worst day of your life?" I asked, and I could hear Parker: *The best day of your life?* The stories we tell ourselves can feel like a weapon to someone else. He didn't look at me, and didn't answer the question.

"Do you know who my dad is?" I asked.

"I wish I did," he said. "You have a right to know. You really do. I can tell you what your mom told me—that she'd met a guy at a conference and they'd had a one-night stand—and maybe that's true."

He shifted creakily and I thought about his former body, trapped inside this older, broken-down one. I could still see the muscles in his arms, the smooth skin on his forehead.

"I wish I knew for sure," I said, avoiding his eyes.

"You have the right to have a father. I really believe that."

My eyelid twitched. "I know," I said. It was my most intimate truth and one, strangely, he knew better than anyone.

They turned the music off, took our cups, and so I struggled into my coat. "Well," I said to the air.

"Wait," he took a breath. I could see him gearing up, and I didn't have time to stop it. "I want to tell you something."

I didn't want him to say it because I wasn't ready, that's the thing. Later, when I started boxing with a trainer in Providence, I had the feeling again. Sometimes you throw this great uppercut and the other guy dodges it and catches you off-balance with a perfect hook anyway.

"I'm sorry about what I did to you." The words came out stilted, just as they had so many years ago. "You didn't deserve it." I knew that I could decide this time if they were real or not, that every moment was a decision, a story you told yourself.

"Okay."

"And I live with the shame of it every day."

We stared at each other. I felt exhausted as if I'd spent the last hour playing rope-a-dope, and he'd startled awake just in time to nail me.

"Well," I tried. I couldn't get past it, couldn't say *I believe you*.

"It's probably unfair to ask you for forgiveness—"

"It is," I said, rallying.

He looked up and maybe his eyes were wet, or maybe I just wanted them to be.

"I'm not sure what forgiveness looks like," I said, "but you should know that I'm alright. I'm happy." Just as I said it, I realized that it was true.

The world is vicious and beautiful and, to some extent, unexplainable. But that doesn't stop us from wanting a story, all the same.

"You probably don't know why you did it," I said, but it came out like a question.

I could see him calculating how much to say, but the

answer wasn't the point. I was in the heart of the matter; I was the kind of man that refused to make another one a monster. I realized I liked who I'd become. It was precisely the feeling I'd been chasing since that night in April when I'd found myself with a gun trained on my back. I could outrun time, I could let my body deliver me, I could trust its instincts. I could know myself.

"Okay," he said, deciding. "I think it was a combination of heavy drinking—I drank so much back then, because I was so stressed about what was going on with your mom and I."

A parade of screwdrivers passed before me: in the car, at dinner, on Christmas morning, after work; but he wasn't a drunk, not the falling-down type, anyway. Maybe he was just a man always looking for something to blame. I swatted his words away, focused. I waited for him to tell the truth.

"And, also, I wasn't molested, exactly," his voice was so soft I could barely hear; breathy, high-pitched. The difference was alarming, and I had a second where I thought maybe he was talking to himself. "But I saw things growing up on the farm that no kid should have to see."

I watched his face pinken, his skin much lighter than mine. I was right, I thought, dumbly.

"I know you like your Uncle John a lot, but he's not a good person."

My heart pounded in my ears. "What do you mean?'

"When we were kids, we'd hang out with all these cousins on our farm." He sucked in his breath, gathered his voice into something more solid. "I remember very clearly being four and John being nine, and these three male cousins having sex with a female cousin in front of us. It happened all the time, they'd all do it. Brother and sister, even."

"Whoa," I exhaled. I could hear the college kids washing dishes and goofing around in the back of the tea shop. "Why is John a bad person?" I asked, not sure I wanted to know. I thought of my mom, how she blamed herself for not sniffing out Roy from the start. There's no metal detector, I wished I could tell her. These people who do the worst things belong to all of us as much as the good guys do.

"John was part of it," he said. He looked away. "He was involved."

John was only a few years older than Roy, which would've made him a victim, too, but I didn't need to say that. I wondered instead about his other family secrets, his Uncle Roy, the stories he didn't want to tell. Everyone is entitled to his own truth, his quiet dignity; even those who try to steal yours.

"Well, I'm really sorry that happened to you," I said.

He looked far away, and I wasn't sure he heard me. "You know," he said, "your mom asked me if I was ever molested and I told her I wasn't, which is true. But I think that this was a form of abuse."

He met my eyes, and I realized that it was a question, that he'd probably not ever asked another person, that he'd probably held this in his gut his whole life. Now, with me, he was finally showing his belly. It would be so easy to stick the knife in and twist it.

"Definitely," I told him. "That's abuse."

"Yeah," he said. "I think so, too."

I thought he'd leave it at that. "No matter what, you didn't deserve what I did to you." I marked, for the first time, that he'd said the word over and over. *Deserve.* I wished I could say that he didn't deserve it, either, but he'd have to figure that out for himself.

"You should know I've never done it before or since. And I've become a better person, I've worked really hard at it."

"Roy?" He looked like I might hit him. "I have always only wanted you to do some good in the world. I mean it. Don't let your whole life be about this."

"Okay." He looked confused. "Like what?"

I tried not to show how deflated I felt. I'd not considered he might miss the point. "Just, you know, find something you care about and do it."

"Okay," he said. "Maybe you could send me some ideas, over email or something?"

I squeezed my eyes shut and opened them again. "Yeah, maybe," I said, finally. "I should get going."

"Long drive tomorrow," he answered, and I let him pretend, just for the moment, that was the reason. We pushed through the shop's glass door into the brisk night, and stood for a second at the corner.

"Take care of yourself," he said, shaking my hand.

"Do something good." I jingled my keys, and we paused in a friendlier freeze. This kind of time could be organic, too, I realized. Time wasn't created in equal portions; memory elongated certain moments and forgot others. My mind wanted to remember this, and his probably did, too.

"'Bye, Roy," I said, finally breaking the spell.

"Hey," he called after me, "write me someday, okay?"

Never, I thought.

"Maybe I will," I said.

He grinned at that, and gave a jolly wave. I watched him recede into the fog, thinking that allowing him this moment was, in all the ways that matter, a kind of forgiveness.

36

Bend, Oregon

June 2011 • 30 years old

I woke to the Little Leaguers outside the motel room, running their mad circles, welcoming the morning like screeching birds. *I'm alive!* they tweeted, back and forth, *I'm alive!*

Parker looked over at me. She smelled of ocean and wet pavement and the familiar spice of morning breath. I wondered how I'd smell once I was on testosterone, if I'd be muskier to her, less sweet.

"How you feeling?" she asked. I didn't answer, just hopped out of bed to open the blinds, watched the boys outside in their red jerseys, going nuts.

"Kind of like that," I said.

"Yeah?"

"Best day of my life," I said, and she laughed but she also knew I meant it.

Last night she'd been in top form, expansive and kind as I'd told her what had transpired, not once offering advice or asking what it all meant, only pulling me to her when I was done. "I'm proud of you," she'd said, letting me rest in the quiet hum of the air conditioner and the thud of her chest. Soon I'd fallen into a clear-headed sleep, experiencing the happy nothingness I'm told children have before drifting off to dreams that don't feature a sweaty father rising at the foot of the bed.

We packed up the car and headed into town to buy two huge iced coffees not far from where I'd met Roy. The sun was bright, hard and hot on my skin, the bite of fog burned off for now.

"Want to get going?" Parker asked, pastry in hand, the morning young and a 10-hour drive to Salt Lake on the docket.

We walked down the side street I'd parked on the night before and then past the tea shop, where the same pierced guy stood at the register, counting out one-dollar bills. He looked up at us, but I couldn't say if he recognized me. On the corner where I'd last seen Roy, a gaggle of men in ties waited for the light to turn so they could cross.

Maybe I'd go to his funeral after all, I thought. Maybe I'd show up in this town a new man in a tailored suit, and be the kind of son who buries his father.

"Road trip!" Parker said, sliding on her sunglasses. The world was strange and we were strangers to so much of it, I thought, and yet here we were, climbing into the hatchback, making ourselves known. I flipped us into reverse, and she studied the directions and reported them to me.

"Go east, young man!" she commanded, hyped up on coffee and the prospect of adventure.

"What?" she said, catching my corny expression.

"You know," I said.

I saw the corners of her lips move to a smile, even as she tried to hide it. So I stayed in my blurring body, an invisible man filling himself in, as we joined the line of cars moving toward the smelly, grassy cow towns, the purple mountains, the power plants, the cornfields, the trailer parks, the red desert—the truth of our united states. I felt I could hold all of it, I was all of it. I was already, always home.

V Man Alive

37

Road Trip

June 2011 • 30 years old

Once we crossed into Wyoming, my mornings took on the same dreamlike, ritualized quality they had on my trip to South Carolina. I suited up in plain T-shirts and blue jeans, sprayed my periphery with cologne, and kept my cap on and my head down. I didn't engage more than I needed to with gas station clerks, toll takers, bartenders.

If Parker was nervous about my safety she didn't tell me so. We rolled through tumbleweed towns and she went inside on her own to buy us bottles of water or to check into the hotel. If she felt lonely or resentful, she kept that quiet too, but I'd feel a little rush of sadness and fear each time she hopped back into the car. How long would she remain my translator? At what point would I look enough like the man I was becoming that I wouldn't need my partner to act as camouflage?

In the bubble of our coffee-cup-filled car, I felt comfortable, familiar. I could predict what would inspire Parker's awe: an antelope perched alongside the empty highway, the makeshift trailer bar with the hand-painted sign, the craggy mountains we drove through at sunset when we veered into Colorado.

But each morning, I gave myself a hard look in the scratched mirrors in Fort Collins or Lincoln or Iowa City, because the 10th of the month was the date of my first shot of testosterone, less than a week away. For the first time in my life, I wasn't "passing" as a man, I was becoming one.

In more anxious moments, washing my hands in single-stall gas station johns, I hoped that being a man would not feel like pretending. I looked in the mirror and tried to imagine myself into being.

I could have a deep voice or a reedy one, I could become bald or not, I could be skinny or muscular, hairy or pimply. I was a mystery to myself, and yet my body knew what it needed. My body waited for me.

◆

After a few days of cowboy side-eye, I got a churn in my gut each time I pushed through the men's room door. I'd sweep the area for boots or beards, keep an eye on whoever eyed me as I head for the stalls. I remembered the fences back near Laramie where Matthew Shepard had been strung up.

Huggins didn't kill me, but someone else could. Each time I stepped into a sticky bar bathroom I knew that, just as I'd known as a child that it doesn't matter why a person tries to destroy you. Being human means being at the mercy of others. It's uncomfortable at that knife's edge, but you've still got a choice about who dictates how you live.

"Tell me something," Parker said, as we passed the town where Brandon Teena, the trans man murdered so many years ago, was buried. "Why do you think he kept living out here? He could've moved to a city. Maybe he'd still be alive if he had."

It was dusky and dry out. For miles we'd seen nothing but the occasional pick-up and the enormous, drooping sky.

"He liked it here?"

She looked around doubtfully.

"Or, I don't know. Maybe he didn't want to be forced to leave in order to be himself," I said.

She looked straight ahead. I didn't know what I was talking about: I'd left Pittsburgh, moved to Boston, to San Francisco, and now I meant to escape again in this move back East. I believed in not getting stuck. I didn't want to end up destroyed by my allegiances to who I thought I should be, or where I expected my life to go. What makes a man? A man makes himself.

Parker bit her lip, and I figured she probably was thinking about how she'd saved up after high school, working a shit job at the mall, so she could leave. Sometimes knowing when to go is the only choice you have.

"I think that's pointless," she said with hard finality.

"I think it's brave, in a way." And I did. "To commit to yourself despite the threat of where you are, to stand your ground in that way."

"It just makes me sad," she said, finally. We were quiet, in agreement that no one should have to be brave in that way.

I could see him, under the biggest sky in the country, weakly counting stars. He was brave because he understood what I was just coming to understand: it's not about nobody ever harming you.

It's about going on, despite it all, knowing that there's part of you that cannot be harmed.

38

New England

Summer 2011 • 30 years old

It wasn't what I expected: not the swiftness in which *ma'am* was replaced with *bro*; not the ease with which men turned to me, expectantly, with long-neck bottles of beer or financial advice; not the way their wives turned away, either.

I didn't expect the electric quality of testosterone, or the near-constant tingle of irritation, the mysterious leg cramps, the quick bloom of my beard, the surge of muscle that rippled through my arms with each new set of pull-ups.

I didn't expect the needles, which were menacingly long, a couple of inches, or the oily amber of the hormone, or the way my life would grow increasingly institutionalized by the blood work and biohazard sharps bins.

I didn't expect the visceral pleasure, either; the joy I found laying a hand on my rising pecs or lifting my shirt to study the hard center of my abs. I didn't expect the shift in my center of gravity or the calf muscles so big they brushed against my pants. I didn't expect the calm at the core of me, my strength a tactile feeling, cool and placid as a lake.

What kind of man was I? I didn't expect how hard it would be to tell, how sweaty and tender the process would be, how often I answered, "I'm doing great!" and smiled wide because I didn't know how to explain the more complex reality: the way I'd catch myself, squaring, in the reflection of my kitchen window at night around midnight when the moon was just so, how I felt like my teenage self in those dressing rooms except that the body I saw now was really mine, no more imagining. And yet I retreated from the beer-breathed New England dudes, friendly guys who connected in their blunted, staccato fashion about sports and vacation plans.

Meanwhile, gay men, sensing my difference, hit on me in dark bars, only to baffle us both.

Parker bought me my first shaving kit and rubbed her hand along my whiskered jaw, but I could feel a part of her shrink as I grew broader. The changes came too fast, like haywire baseballs in a batting cage, and each night I'd come home from my day job at a newspaper, exhausted and restless, she'd keep track of each hair, as if mapping me would keep me familiar.

Both of us insisted that we weren't beginning again until it became clear that we were doing exactly that.

Parker, lying on the couch in our new living room, which seemed sprung from our fantasy life with its crown molding and graceful windows, looked at me like a stranger as I asked a million anxious questions: *Why did I care if other men didn't hug, why should that stop me? What if a woman didn't want to be hugged, though, was that oppressive?*

I was afraid. I didn't want to go swimming, didn't want my still-measly chest set alongside hairier ones.

"Now that you're a guy, talking about yourself all the time means something different," Parker said. The exhaustion in her voice scared me.

"You don't know what it's like!" I could hear myself

yelling, but I was not the man whose vein pulsed in helpless rage, I wasn't the kind of man who didn't know who he was.

I could feel myself trapped in the wrong story and the right body and she cried and said I was right, she didn't.

39

New England

Summer 2011 • 30 years old

Becoming a man felt bright and bracing, like a cup of strong coffee, all jangly energy and sparks. It felt brutish and graceful, like boxing, the physical dance of my transition.

"It's a ballet," Parker said, watching me jab, duck, hook. It was a relief to finally be understood.

In the muggy heart of summer I accidently cut my hand with the needle while prepping my shot. The harsh red of my blood spread its beauty across my knuckles. It looked violent and felt like that edgy, vital tension that curled my fists in public bathrooms and told me that my body was a castle worth protecting.

Many of my friends were new moms, people as obsessed with their bodies as I was, calculating the changes and their costs, the weight and the baby brain and the indifferent or prescriptive world they were entering. They were afraid and excited and underprepared and universes unto themselves, like me.

Everything felt more vivid those first few months: colors, my own smell, the blare of a gendered faux pas, the sweet and relentless cheerleading of old friends studying me when they thought I wasn't looking. I was an animal free of his shell, exposed in ways I hadn't grown defenses for.

I called my brother, Scott, more than usual. He was the

only man I felt comfortable enough to ask about puberty, and his initial reaction to my transition had erased years of awkwardness and sealed us, magically, in brotherhood. It's funny to think that I'd been sweaty and drinking away my jitters when we met for a beer before I left San Francisco. I wasn't sure why I'd expected him to react poorly—maybe because I'd shied away from Scott as a kid, seeing Roy in his jaw and lean build. Scott alone knew how I'd felt about men, and how wrong I'd been.

He came straight from work that day at a dot-com in Silicon Valley to the dark bar I'd chosen on Valencia, his face turning serious as I said I had something important to tell him. He looked grown, impossibly strong and adult. He laughed in relief after I'd outlined the shots, the changes, the name change. "Okay, that's it?" he said, shaking his head. "I mean, come on. You've always been a guy to me."

So Scott and I exchanged phone calls and talked muscle groups, hormones, his days playing hockey in high school—the aggression, the chemical feel of it. He promised me I'd find balance, told me to go hard, to harness those chemicals for barbells and crunches and planks, to make something strong and good of myself.

"There's no man like you," Parker said, and of course she was right but I also thought of Scott, of every good man I knew.

Parker and I lay in our backyard under the fir tree on the hammock we'd bought in Mexico, our bodies as suspended as our lives. She squinted at me and I kissed her freckled nose, thinking that our honeymoon had happened to a different body. It had and it hadn't, and I knew right then that living with that reality was going to be the hardest part.

No man like me. I was a trans man, an invisible man.

I'd have to make peace with not being able to be all of my selves at once.

I breathed in the smell of us, our coconut lotion, flicked away the same mosquitoes I'd known since I was a kid—but the world felt different, tilted.

I could only be my own man; I didn't have a choice.

◆

"Your voice!" Mom said, winded but enthusiastic. "You sound just like your uncles."

I knew she'd run up the carpeted stairs when she'd seen the caller ID, my name probably changed but who knows. Part of why I'd waited so long to call, if I admitted it to myself, was that I was afraid it wasn't, afraid I'd never be Thomas to her.

"How's Grandma?" I asked. Last I heard, Grandma thought she was going on a trip, by boat, to New Orleans, waving goodbye to all of her friends on the banks. I softened at the thought of the two of them: Mom, the grown-up scientist, showing her own mom family pictures in the dementia unit.

"She's alright. Better at the new place."

There was a sad silence. I gathered Grandma hadn't been the easiest mother: she could be fierce and protective, but she was edgy and distant, too. I could feel Mom's grief, frozen like that icicle on the window of my college apartment.

"Most people don't have both parents alive as long as I have," she said, as if continuing a conversation we'd started long ago. "I'm lucky. I'm 67 years old, for god's sake."

"I'm sorry, Mom." I tried to think of anything but her

death. If you didn't count her voicemail, we'd not spoken in months, not since my letter back in February went unanswered, not since I saw Roy. We'd sent a few quick, tentative emails in recent weeks, all of them building up to this.

Slowly, as the summer sparkled on, it had occurred to me how much I'd missed her.

Outside, lawnmowers whirred their summer prayer. A cardinal and I locked eyes through the kitchen window until a troop of neighborhood kids, screaming their unintelligible glory, ran by and scared it off.

"Anyway, I read your letter," she said, changing course. I knew she was probably wiping away tears with the back of her hand; she could cry without making a sound. "So what do you want to know?"

I suddenly didn't care about any of it, but I pressed on. If I buckled now, I'd never discover some crucial part of myself—not where I came from, exactly, but who I was in the face of it.

"I know this is probably hard for you," I said, and she didn't answer. "I just want to know the whole story."

"Whatever you want, I'll tell you," she said, her voice small. I studied my reflection in the window. I'd only ever looked when the moon blurred me mysteriously, not under the strange glare of the sun. This was a different picture: the red dots of acne, the wayward cowlick, the whole truth. Still, I didn't turn away.

"Where should I start?" she asked.

"The beginning," I told her, thinking of her own birth, or Grandma's, but knowing that she was my mother, so she'd start, as always, with me.

◆

"You have to understand: I just wanted to get pregnant, you know? I was getting a divorce, I was 36. At that point, I didn't care about there being a father."

I tried to make acknowledging sounds, tried not to ignore the whoosh that rattled my chest even if I wanted it gone. I reminded myself of all my single friends in their thirties who'd said the same thing to me, women who'd sworn they'd give their kid twice as much love to make up the difference.

"But, Mom, what if I'd wanted a father?"

I could hear the shock in her silence. "Well, I didn't think about that," she said. "I guess I should have."

"You should have," I told her, a little steel in my tone.

"I didn't think I'd find a man I wanted to be with, I'd kind of given up on them, honestly. I thought I would just have you and be a single mom, that was the plan. I should have stuck to it."

For the first time in my life, I didn't feel the need to reassure her. She could feel what she wanted; it was her story, not mine, after all.

"So what happened?"

"I started dating Roy, very casually. I met Jim at a conference not long after, and he and I were only together once. Roy and I were very informal, so it didn't seem like a big deal."

"Then you and Roy got serious?"

"Correct," she said, assuming her scientist voice. "When I found out I was pregnant, I figured you had to be his."

"But—" This was the axis her story spun on, and I almost said so, but it felt mean. She already knew where it had fallen apart.

"I didn't mean it to be hurtful," she said quietly. Watching a parent humble herself is like one of those nature shows about lion fights. I flashed on the sorry feeling I always got when the losing lion put its head down and backed away.

"I know, Mom," I said.

"I just keep thinking about the day you were born," she said. "They did the C-section and just handed you over the surgical partition. You looked right at me," she said dreamily.

I'd never understand what it was to imagine a baby into being, but I did know something about the miracle of making a man where there wasn't one.

"What do you think I saw?"

"I don't know," she said. "But you wouldn't look away."

I was Thomas right now, I realized, but also her Pip. And I was finally unburdening myself of my great expectations.

I kept my eyes on the backyard, the hammock swinging as if holding a ghost. Through the window, I watched as the cardinal moved on, and then a bluebird appeared—a parade of birds from my childhood.

"I wish you'd had a different life," she said. It was a familiar refrain, the sour note underscoring every great occasion.

"I don't," I said, surprised again at the steel in my voice—a circle I made around myself, a glinting, warning blade. "Mom, every time you say that, I feel like you're missing the life I've got."

"I'm not!" she said. And then, more thoughtfully, "I'm so proud of you."

She was, I knew. She was here, in my story, after all.

"I know you've forgiven him," she sighed, "I don't know how you've done it. I just don't think I ever could."

She wasn't exactly right, but I didn't say so. "That's your business. I don't think you have to."

"It's just, I loved him," she sounded surprised at herself. "It seems hard to believe now, but I did."

"I know."

"You do?"

"Yeah, Mom, of course."

"Oh."

The cardinal returned, calling out as it hopped from branch to branch. The guys working on the roof next door blasted AC/DC and hammered, shirtless and half-drunk, in short bursts.

"So what do you think of having another son?"

She laughed, and I could sense her relief. "I'm not surprised," she said. "I'm happy if you're happy."

And that's the truth: she always was.

"Let me ask you something," she said.

"Sure."

"Growing up," she asked carefully, "did you know that I loved you?"

I could tell this was bigger than me—about Grandma, maybe; or about all the failures that lead, in the end, to success.

Hadn't she, in so many ways, delivered me here?

Did I know I was loved?

"Of course," I said. I'd never doubted it, and she was right—that, in the end, was measure enough.

New England

September 2011 • 30 years old

"We have to let each other change," Parker said as I flipped turkey burgers in the backyard. It was late summer, though our shadows seemed to grow shorter each day.

"I know." I didn't, though, not exactly. As I was sorting out the basics of moving my body through space, she'd gained a different sparkle—she, too, was a twin of herself.

"I feel like I keep waiting for you to go back to being the way you were before," she said, and I looked up to see if she meant it. She didn't meet my eyes.

"Oh."

The stars weren't out yet, but the night was buggy and growing worse. Parker was sweet, her mom told me, so she got bit first. It was always true, even if it was the kind of thing a mom would say.

"I think I'm waiting for the same thing," I said, closing the lid and sitting down beside her at our landlord's picnic table.

"You're waiting to return to normal or for me to?"

"Both."

It felt good to say it, to look around the foreign yard with its hammock and garden, to hold the hand of the woman I used to understand in a body that didn't quite feel like my own and to admit I was lost.

"You can't really plan for anything, can you?" I asked. "I mean you can change the story you tell yourself, but the truth is you've still got to just let everything unfold and see what happens next."

"It's like the ocean," she said, and smiled tightly.

"I miss how we used to be."

"Me too," she said. The cicadas sawed on in their relentless drone. I twisted the ring around my finger; reassured by its weight and the way it circled my bone. "But you have to let me change, too." She laughed sharply. "I'm transitioning."

"You're angry."

My legs were hairier than they'd ever been, and I studied the swirls covering my exposed thighs. Parker, thinking something similar maybe, ran her finger through the forest of my shin.

"I miss you, but I like the new you, too. You're Thomas."

"I don't even know what that means yet."

"You will."

The turkey sizzled and popped, so I flipped the patties and sat back down. I thought about Mom, about Roy, about the ways she was part of why I wasn't like him, regardless of blood. Parker sipped her beer contemplatively, wrapped in a sweatshirt, as if in anticipation of autumn.

"Do you feel loved?" I asked.

She looked at me, surprised, and I saw every Parker then: the girl I got drunk with in college, the baby-faced woman whose apartment I moved into in Oakland, the girlfriend so scared driving me to top surgery in San Francisco that she had to pull over to retch on the side of the road, the partner in the purple dress pouring champagne in Mendocino, the person with the big eyes and the full heart that transcended every incarnation, just like me.

"What do you mean?" She swatted at her legs and caught a swollen mosquito.

"Do you feel loved?" I repeated. She picked at her shorts and considered it.

"Yeah, I feel loved," she said softly. "Do you?"

We looked up at the same stars we'd seen for seven years together, the same stars I'd seen since I started keeping track back in elementary school. There was the Big Dipper, the constellation I'd looked for each night before going back inside after smoking a cigarette in college—a ritual, a promise that I was still here.

"I do," I said, making a different kind of vow, the kind that could never be broken, true and intangible as the moment.

◆

That weekend we went to Plum Island despite the slight chill in the air, not ready to surrender to it. Parker lay back in her spotted bikini, and I sat up in my T-shirt and watched the horizon, thinking of Mexico.

"What?" she asked, and I shook my head. "You swimming today?"

"Next time," I said. I knew there wouldn't be a next time for another year now that the leaves were turning. I'd spotted a couple tattooed guys with cans of beer downwind and didn't want any trouble today. Shirtless, I didn't quite pass. I looked androgynous, a little untranslatable.

"Suit yourself," she said. I didn't have to remind her of that day in Tulum. I did want to get in the water, but didn't want to end up crawling out of it again.

She hopped up and tossed her sunglasses down on the blanket, powered by that old purposeful hum. I watched her charge the water like it belonged to her, and it made me want to stand up and cheer.

I looked down at my tan body, my new self. The muscles of my calves bulged gently outward and I touched them as if to scan for the feeling of running down 41st Street, but of course it wasn't located there. What I wanted was the part of me that knew what to do; that knowledge didn't live anywhere in particular. It was everywhere.

I looked up in time to catch Parker aiming her body gracefully into a slip of wave. She popped out, like a seal, on the other side of it.

I stood up and let the breeze ruffle my shirt like a flag. It was the last day of summer, no doubt.

By next year, I'd be Thomas, no longer between selves. But for now I was only exactly the man I was, smooth and hairless around my pecs.

I watched Parker pitch herself a few more times into the waves before turning on her back to float. Always something to prove, I thought affectionately, but underneath she knew exactly when to let go.

The wind caught my T-shirt and it billowed out and in again, shifting my form. Horizons looked both finite and endless. They were the place that allowed a long view, an ending and a beginning at once.

I walked toward Parker, who lifted her head and caught sight of me just as I pulled off my shirt. My skin pimpled against the salty air, my body automatic, changing, alive.

"Hey," Parker called, "you're here!"

"I'm here," I yelled back, holding my shirt above my

head and sloshing through the tide without any of her grace but with my own insistent force. I ran until the water slowed me; until Parker and the horizon disappeared; until all I could see was a gathering wave; until all I could do was dive.

ACKNOWLEDGMENTS

I'm so grateful to Elaine Katzenberger, Chris Carosi, and Stacey Lewis at City Lights and to Michelle Tea for believing in my book and being relentless champions of my work. I'm indebted to Chris Tomasino, my agent, for her dogged efforts on my behalf, her sharp edits, and for focusing me on what matters most in my work, every time. I owe Emma Larson, her former assistant, a big thank-you for finding me more than two years ago and for helping usher me onto this journey in the first place.

Thanks to the San Francisco Foundation, whose support was crucial to this project. A big thank you to RADAR Productions, an organization that's supported me in more ways than I can count.

Without the Rumpus and the opportunity they've given me to write my column, "Self-Made Man," I wouldn't only be a lesser writer, I've no doubt I'd not be the man I am today. Thank you to Stephen Elliott, Isaac Fitzgerald, Zoe Ruiz, and most especially my editor, Julie Greicius, who may know me better than I know myself.

I'm tremendously indebted to my artistic community, who gave me notes and came to my readings and invited me to read and bought me drinks and published me and promoted my work and cheerled me with big, kind hearts: Michelle Carter, Donna de la Perrière, Alex Dumont, Anisse Gross, Kevin Hobson, Saeed Jones, Katie Liederman, Carrie Leilam Love, Tuck Mayo, Annie Mebane, Toni Mirosevich, Lauren Morelli, Rachel Nelson, Elizabeth Scarboro, Sara Seinberg, Ana Ventura, Danielle Vogel, Ketch Wehr, Eugenia Williamson, Carlin Wing, Kareem Worrell, and Heather Woodward. I wish I had room to name every person who's been a part of this project in some way, but know that whatever you did for me, I'm grateful.

Thanks to my many students, who've taught me how to write.

A very special thanks to Emily Carlson, who is a brilliant poet, my oldest friend, and whose many, many edits pushed me to make this book glow.

Thanks to Xavier Schipani for his beautiful cover illustration, and his friendship.

Thanks to Jessica McCarthy, for seeing clear through from day one. You've changed everything.

Thanks to my family for loving me for the brother and son and writer I am, and for their grace in allowing me to write about our lives, even the hard parts.

And a huge gratitude to Michael Braithwaite: for her endless support, her friendship, and her sass; but mostly for showing me how to be family, and for teaching me that it's like the ocean. It really, really is.

ABOUT THE AUTHOR

Thomas Page McBee was the "masculinity expert" for *VICE* and writes the columns "Self-Made Man" for *the Rumpus* and "The American Man" for *Pacific Standard*. His essays and reportage have appeared in the *New York Times*, The-Atlantic.com, *Salon*, and *Buzzfeed*, where he was a regular contributor on gender issues. He lives in New York City where he works as the editor of special projects at Quartz, and is currently at work on a book about modern American masculinity.